the DECODING the DISCIPLINES PARADIGM

SCHOLARSHIP OF TEACHING AND LEARNING

Jennifer Meta Robinson, Whitney M. Schlegel, and Mary Taylor Huber, editors

the DECODING the DISCIPLINES PARADIGM

Seven Steps to Increased Student Learning

DAVID PACE

Indiana University Press

Bloomington and Indianapolis

This book is a publication of

Indiana University Press
Office of Scholarly Publishing
Herman B Wells Library 350
1320 East 10th Street
Bloomington, Indiana 47405 USA

iupress.indiana.edu

The paper used in this publication meets the minimum
requirements of the American National Standard for Information
Sciences—Permanence of Paper for Printed Library Materials,
ANSI Z39.48-1992.

Manufactured in the United States of America

Cataloging information is available from the Library of Congress.

ISBN 978-0-253-02453-4 (cloth)
ISBN 978-0-253-02458-9 (paperback)
ISBN 978-0-253-02465-7 (ebook)

1 2 3 4 5 22 21 20 19 18 17

To those who are at the core of everything I do:
Georg'ann, Kate, and Griffin

Contents

Preface and Acknowledgments

AUTHORSHIP IS SUCH a troubled concept. Our cultural traditions require a hero, just as our sociopolitical system focuses attention on the lone entrepreneur. Thus, we place a name on the cover of every book and imagine an author, operating in isolation, who brought a set of ideas into existence ex nihilo. But such moments of solitary creation are, at most, relatively rare occurrences. We are a social species, and we think best when we think together.

These considerations are particularly relevant at the beginning of this book, because the *we* behind it is much more powerful than the *I*. The community that contributed to its creation has numbered well over a hundred people, but at the core of this effort was the impressive work of Joan Middendorf, who worked alongside me to create the Freshman Learning Project (FLP) at Indiana University–Bloomington, and of Arlene Díaz and Leah Shopkow, who joined us in IU's History Learning Project (HLP). And beyond that inner circle, the faculty fellows and the PhD students who worked with the FLP and the HLP made great contributions to the development of the Decoding the Disciplines process. The many participants in workshops around the world contributed examples and participated in the interview process; more recently, teams of scholars of teaching and learning at other universities around the world are moving the approach beyond its original limits.

At every moment from its conception to its emergence as a complex, articulated approach to facilitating learning, this has been a shared project. A comment by a fellow in the FLP might set in motion a chain of thoughts that began to take shape months later over a luncheon of the HLP; that conversation generated a classroom lesson in one of our courses that led to the formulation of a new principle, and a question from the audience at a workshop in another country provided a metaphor that nailed down the concept. Thus, it should never be assumed that everything in this book that is not specifically ascribed to one of my colleagues is the result of my individual ruminations.

Within this shared conceptual space we have each brought special experiences and skills to the table that have allowed our team to gain insights that would most likely have been impossible to attain in isolation. As time has passed, however, we have come to see decoding in somewhat different ways and to describe it in slightly different language. Thus, there is nothing canonical about the precise form of decoding as it is presented in this book. Others in our team would have used different metaphors and examples, emphasized different aspects of the process, and in some cases drawn different conclusions. This is already visible in the work that we have produced and will undoubtedly be even more visible in the future. This is a sign of the vitality and richness of the approach, and any attempt to impose an orthodoxy on decoding will only weaken it.

More than a decade has passed since the Decoding the Disciplines process was introduced in a special issue of the journal *New Directions for Teaching and Learning* in 2004. The paradigm has expanded in so many directions in the intervening years that it is time to draw together the ideas and strategies that have emerged since that publication. In addition to my work, Joan Middendorf and Leah Shopkow will be publishing *Decoding the Disciplines: How to Help Students Learn Critical Thinking,* a practical introduction to the decoding process, in which instructors and educational developers will be presented with the concrete steps needed to implement this approach in courses and in the scholarship of teaching and learning. Leah, Joan, Arlene, and I are working on a detailed study in which we will use decoding to examine teaching and learning history. A team at Mount Royal University, including Jennifer Boman, Genevieve Currie, Ron MacDonald, Janice Miller-Young, Michelle Yeo, and Stephanie Zettel, have produced *Using the Decoding the Disciplines Framework for Learning across Disciplines,* another volume on the application of the decoding paradigm, which will appear in the *New Directions for Teaching and Learning* series, and scholars of teaching throughout the world are generating presentations and articles that further articulate the model.

My own chief contribution to this literature is the present volume. The choice of words, the emphasis, and in many cases the particular spin given to Decoding the Disciplines in the pages that follow are mine, and I take full responsibility for any errors of reasoning or infelicities of presentation that may have occurred in the writing of this work. But, while the words that follow are mine, very few of them would have found their way to the page without a process of collective reasoning and exploration over the last decade. I have gained more than I can express from this community, and what I have learned from my collaborators has been the greatest gift that I have received in my professional life.

As a historian, I can best represent the nature of this shared enterprise by offering a brief history of Decoding the Disciplines. I am writing, of necessity from a limited perspective, and I am certain that I have not done justice to the contributions of all those who have been involved. But, I believe that it is important to provide readers with some sense of the process by which these ideas developed. (Readers who are not so inflicted with historicity may feel free to skip to the book's introduction, though they should be warned that an understanding of the basic challenges that brought us to this work may help in understanding its implications.)

My Personal Journey to Decoding

My path to this book began in the spring of 1988, when I was jolted out of pedagogical complacency by a single sentence uttered by Craig Nelson. Craig is one of
the elder sages of the world of teaching, and I have had the privilege of learning
from him for four decades. But at that particular moment he simply pointed out
that most of what we call teaching is really sorting. Students who have been "preeducated" are praised and judged to be worthy, whereas those who arrive with
more minimal preparation are dismissed as lazy or stupid. Teaching, by contrast,
would involve actually giving students the tools that they need to succeed in our
disciplines.

Before that moment I had had some sense of the injustice that resulted from
ineffective teaching, but the clarity and precision of this comment caused a great
deal of soul searching on my part. I had to admit that, despite a decade and a half
of working on my teaching of history courses at Indiana University Bloomington, I, too, was still sorting students. I had already begun to explore literature on
learning, and I suspected that something as simple as responding to phrases such
as "compare and contrast" or "support this argument" required cognitive abilities that had not been cultivated in many of my students. My exams required the
kind of complex mental operations that William Perry's work (1970) had demonstrated were only mastered by most students in their later years at Harvard
University. And yet I was assuming mastery of such abilities in courses at a large
state university.

I had to face the fact that in my own role as a teacher I was reinforcing all the
inequalities that I deplored in rants about the injustice of our society. Students
arrived at the door of my classroom with radically different levels of preparation.
The children of privilege had been "preeducated" and would succeed in society
no matter what occurred in my course. But others had suffered from years of
pedagogical neglect and were ill-prepared for the challenges they will face in my
course. By requiring skills that I was not teaching, I was inadvertently reinforcing
and legitimizing the notion that some of my students counted and others did not.

This realization left me with a dilemma: I seemed to be faced with a choice
between forsaking the material and the ideas I wanted to teach or abandoning
many of my students and reinforcing the inequality of opportunity that I found
repellent. Thus, the only ethically acceptable choice was to follow the old Yiddish
proverb: when someone offers you two choices, pick the third. That third alternative seemed to be to create some mechanism within my courses that would allow
at least some of my students to master those basic mental operations that they
had not been taught earlier but which were needed for success in my course. I
produced a user's guide for my survey of modern European history that presented students with some of the basic ways of operating in a history course and
provided examples of how to select what was important to remember in the readings

or lectures and how to go about writing an essay exam (Pace 1993). I developed these ideas somewhat in the sections I wrote in *Studying for History*, a work for undergraduates in introductory history courses that I coauthored with Sharon Pugh (Pace and Pugh 1995).

But all of this remained unclear, confused, and focused entirely on history until Joan Middendorf, then director of IU's Teaching Resources Center, asked me to join her in the first Indiana University Leadership Institute. This brilliantly conceived and executed eight-day program, designed by Eileen Bender, Barbara Cambridge, Pat Hutchings, and Susan Sciame-Giesecke helped Joan and me to turn a vague idea into a rough idea for a program that would help faculty define the mental operations required for success in their courses and develop more effective ways to teach these skills to undergraduates. We received support and intellectual input from a number of administrators, including Bob Orsi, Pam Walters and, most notably, Ray Smith, who played a key role in the conceptualization and implementation of what became the FLP.

The partnership with Joan quickly deepened as she applied her expertise in the dissemination of ideas to the concrete problem of creating a faculty development program aimed at providing a framework within which instructors could identify the basic mental operations required in their courses and then systematically model these for their students (Middendorf 1999). With financial support from a special fund set up by Indiana University president Miles Brand, the first group of FLP faculty fellows met in May 1998.

For the next dozen years the FLP provided Joan and me with a laboratory within which we could explore ways to increase student learning in a wide range of disciplines. The dedicated and insightful faculty fellows who participated in the program played a crucial role in all of this, through their suggestions and objections and through the marvelous model lessons they shared with the group. Ray Smith continued to work tirelessly and at some personal sacrifice to obtain funds for the program first through the Lilly Retention Initiative and then through the IU Dean of Faculties Office. And Gregor Novak, who was developing Just-in-Time Teaching fifty miles away in Indianapolis, generously contributed his time and insights to our work. Over the years the outline of the Decoding the Disciplines process continued as Joan and I added one step after another until the paradigm emerged roughly in its current form.

Meanwhile I had the great privilege of serving as a fellow in the Carnegie Academy for the Scholarship of Teaching and Learning (CASTL), an extraordinary program that jump-started the scholarship of teaching and leaning (SoTL) under the direction of a set of brilliant academic leaders, including Marcia Babb, Barbara Cambridge, Mary Huber, Pat Hutchings, and Lee Shulman; my debt to these visionaries and to those in my CASTL cohort is immense. This experience provided me with a deeper understanding of the nature and importance of SoTL at the same time that it linked me to a network of scholars that has been invaluable in the development and dissemination of decoding.

The CASTL experience and the activity on our campus which contributed to the formation of the International Society for the Scholarship of Teaching and Learning (ISSOTL), caused a shift in the focus of decoding. It had originally been conceptualized primarily as a faculty development program aimed at helping instructors find better ways to help students master difficult aspects of specific disciplines, but in the early part of the new millennium, Joan and I increasingly realized that it could also serve as a platform for research into teaching and learning. This realization led directly to the publication of *Decoding the Disciplines: Helping Students Learn Disciplinary Ways of Thinking* (Pace and Middendorf 2004), in which FLP fellows shared their efforts to use this approach to increase learning in a variety of fields.

In the decade that followed we had the opportunity to share the continuing development of the decoding paradigm through articles, presentations at scholarly conferences, and workshops at a wide range of universities. These events provided an occasion for numerous exchanges with other academics interested in teaching and learning, and these conversations deepened the practice. But it was clear quite early that for decoding to have maximum impact it would be necessary to systematically explore its use in a particular discipline.

It was at this point that Arlene Díaz and Leah Shopkow joined Joan and me to form the HLP. As professional historians in different subfields, Arlene and Leah brought us greater depth in the discipline. But, more important, they were skilled and committed teachers whose participation as fellows in the FLP had provided them with a solid grounding in decoding. And each brought special skills and concerns. Leah had a strong grounding in the philosophy of history and led us into a much deeper encounter with theoretical issues—in particular, the relationship of decoding to disciplinary epistemologies. Arlene contributed valuable quantitative skills and a focus on the application of decoding to the curricular problems faced by academic departments. But even more important than the specific skills they brought to the process was their involvement in a powerful experience of collaborative reasoning about the nature of learning and strategies for bringing it about.

The newly founded HLP began its work by applying the decoding interview format developed in the FLP (described in chapter 2) to the bottlenecks in learning that appeared in college history courses. With grant support from the Dean of Faculties Office, in 2006 we videotaped interviews with twenty-four colleagues in the IU Department of History. In these interviews we sought to make explicit the steps that students needed to master in order to overcome common obstacles to learning history. The contribution of these historians to the development of decoding was enormous, as they not only shared their wisdom about teaching and learning but also allowed us to probe those areas that remained unclear. Their generosity in participating in the interviews and in allowing us to use excerpts from the videos in presentations has had a major impact on the development and spread of decoding.

In the next stage of the project, with the support of a grant from the Teagle and Spencer Foundations and generous assistance from Robert Thompson, we began the process of analysis and application. Across a three-year period we worked with history department faculty (Michael Grossberg, Padraic Kenny, Marissa Moorman, John Nieto-Phillips, and Eric Sandweiss), PhD students (Keith Eberly, Mayumi Hoshino, Nicole McGrath, Jolanta Mickute, Jose Najar, Lauren Miller Poor, and Tara Saunders), and administrative assistant Catherine Brennan to explore the mental operations revealed in the earlier interviews and to find effective ways to model these in history courses. Joan drew the group into a much more serious engagement with emotional bottlenecks, Leah explored the connections between decoding and threshold concepts, and Arlene led the Department of History in creating an outline for a decoded curriculum.

The work of the HLP, the exploration of decoding in our own classes, and Joan's work with clients in the IU Center for Innovative Teaching and Learning have all deepened the paradigm. But decoding would not have become the robust approach that it is today without the many contributions of our colleagues at Indiana University, especially the commitment, creativity, and feedback of the hundred instructors from our campus who served as faculty fellows in the FLP. Tony Ardizzone, Trudy Banta, Fritz Breithaupt, Richard Durisen, Valerie Grim, Paul Gutjahr, Roger Innes, Shanker Krishnan, Lisa Kurz, Catherine Pilachowski, Barry Rubin, Whitney Schlegel, Susan Strome, and Mimi Zolan really moved this work forward through their articles in *Decoding the Disciplines: Helping Students Learn Disciplinary Ways of Thinking*. Decoding also benefitted greatly from the generosity of members of IU's Department of History (Maria Bucur, Claude Clegg, Nick Cullather, Kon Dierks, Deborah Deliyannis, Wendy Gamber, Peter Guardino, John Hanson, Sarah Knott, Ed Linenthal, Jim Madison, Marissa Moorman, Khalil Muhammad, Amrita Myers, John Nieto-Phillips, Scott O'Bryan, Eric Robinson, Mark Roseman, Eric Sandweiss, Christina Snyder, Lynn Struve, Kristen Sword, and Jeff Veidlinger) and Department of Geological Sciences (Simon Brassell, Jim Brophy, Michael Hamburger, Claudia Johnson, and Chen Zhu), who submitted to a demanding ninety-minute interview process. Their input was a real prerequisite to the progress that has been made in understanding both bottlenecks in learning and the kinds of mental operations that students must master to get past them. Erika Biga Lee has been very generous in her assistance on the further development of the Decoding the Disciplines website, as well as the work she and her colleagues in the School of Informatics and Computing (J. Duncan, Adrian German, and Suzanne Menzel) have done. And once again it is crucial to stress the advice and support of Ray Smith, without whom none of this might have developed.

The development of decoding has, of course, long since moved beyond the boundaries of a single university due to the work of clusters of instructors, educational developers, and scholars of teaching and learning around the world. In addition to the team at Mount Royal University, it is essential to acknowledge the contribution to the enrichment and spread of the model by Andrea Frank, Svenja Kaduk, Swantje Lahm, Klaus Reinhold, Kerrin Riewerts, and Petra Weiss at the University of Bielefeld; Manie Moolman, Deirdre van Jaarsveldt, and Annette Wilkinson at the University of the Free State in Bloemfontein, South Africa; James Cronin and Bettie Higgs at University College Cork; Julie Timmermans at the University of Waterloo; Brad Wuetherick at Dalhousie University; Peter Felton at Elon University; Kimberly de La Harpe and Gregor Novak at the U.S. Air Force Academy; Ali Erkan and Michael Smith at Ithaca College; and Miako Rankin at Gallaudet University. Most recently, Jolanta Mickute at Vytautas Magnus University; Dominique Verpoorte at the University of Liège; and Kathrin Gläser, Kathrin Munt, Peter Riegler, and Sebastian Wirthgen at Ostfalia University of Applied Sciences have all helped further develop and spread the paradigm. Without the insights and questions of all of these people and of many of the hundreds of participants in decoding workshops and presentations this book would be much less rich.

I also have an enormous debt to the broader community of scholars of teaching and learning. Randy Bass, Dan Bernstein, Lendol Calder, Pat Hutchings, Mills Kelly, Sherry Linkon, and so many others, whom I met through the Carnegie Academy for the Scholarship of Teaching and Learning, have continued to serve as a source of inspiration and ideas. Of this group Tony Ciccone, Jennifer Robinson, Whitney Schlegel, and, especially, Mary Huber deserve particular thanks for their suggestions on earlier versions of the manuscript for this book. Alan Booth, Sean Brawley, Keith Erekson, Paul Hyland, Mills Kelly, and Geoff Timmins all help inspire me to keep working on decoding history; they have helped make this a much better piece of work. And I owe a great deal to all those who have invested thousands of hours in maintaining the International Society for the Scholarship of Teaching and Learning, which has been so central to the development of decoding.

Finally, a few very personal thank-yous. I must mention the late Ivan Karp, whose small act of kindness to me decades ago allowed my career to proceed as it has, and Jim Harrison, who has spent the last half century educating me in so many ways. Invaluable multihour luncheons with Christian Briggs opened new possibilities for decoding that I would never have realized on my own. The profound wisdom of Lynn James helped lead this work to a more satisfactory conclusion that I had once imagined possible. And, finally of course, thanks go to Georg'ann

Cattelona, whose importance in this work and in everything that I have done for more than three decades is utterly beyond my powers to express.

I have been so blessed by friends, family, mentors, and so many others who have made my path possible. The present book attempts to draw together the diverse strands of decoding into a coherent thesis in order to make this approach available to a larger audience, but the paradigm has already grown beyond the capacity of any single person to encompass all its facets. Thus, I begin with some trepidation, aware of the massive debts I owe to those with whom I have had the privilege to work, but hopeful that this work will serve to introduce others to an approach that I have found so rewarding.

DECODING *the* DISCIPLINES PARADIGM

INTRODUCTION: AN OVERVIEW OF DECODING THE DISCIPLINES

SOMEWHERE IN THE world at this very moment there is a college class that is not working: an earnest instructor is deeply committed to sharing what makes his or her discipline so compelling, and the class is filled with students who would desperately like to succeed, but the instructor's words are not connecting. The students have no idea what they are actually supposed to do to master the material at hand—or, worse, they are confidently following strategies that are completely inappropriate for the discipline.

For all concerned it is a downward spiral. Once again the students are reminded that it does not much matter what they do; when they put effort into their courses, the results are quite meager. As a result they withdraw, placing their energies elsewhere, in parts of their lives that seem to offer a greater chance of a return. The instructor's response is similar. Once again an investment of time and personal resources in the course has yielded few returns. Aside from a couple of "ringers" who share the teacher's enthusiasm and were already able to function in the discipline before the course began, the class remains an inert mass, seemingly impervious to learning. Each day the instructor feels a little less willing to invest in the course, a little more resentment toward those who "refuse" to learn, and increasingly inclined to transfer more attention to those areas of academic life that offer better chances for success.

This sad story has, of course, been playing out since formal education began. It has led to innumerable microtragedies as students have had their hopes for the future dashed and faculty have seen a major part of their professional identity mired in failure and resentment. But the system has continued to function because society's need for education has been limited. So long as instructors conveyed a stream of knowledge to the small number of future professionals, the system survived. In fact, the failure to educate had a perverse function, since one of the primary roles of college professors was to restrict the awarding of degrees to that relatively small group who had the exceptional abilities, elite preparation, or social connections that marked them as particularly eligible for positions in law, medicine, and other professions.

We are now viewing the death throes of a world in which learning was a luxury item to be enjoyed by the very few. The conception of the instructor as a gatekeeper maintaining the standards of an institution is now being challenged within large sections of higher education. College no longer functions primarily as a finishing school for a relatively small elite and as a passport to a limited number of positions that actually require the skills conveyed in higher education (Horowitz 1987). Higher education has become the primary pathway to a full life as a breadwinner, citizen, and inhabitant of an ever more complex world. Ineffective teaching can prevent many students from ever reaching these goals, and it very often serves to reinforce the other inequalities that have already diminished the possibilities of so many of them. This new situation greatly increases the ethical responsibility of instructors to provide students with a clear pathway into their disciplines.

Changes in the nature of knowledge itself are also disrupting the world of college teaching. As has often been noted, the speed with which knowledge is growing and the ease with which it is available have made obsolete the identification of learning with the memorization of content. There is less reason to teach students facts that will soon be outdated, and that can be summoned in an instant with a few keystrokes. Increasingly, it is the *how to,* not the *what,* that must be transmitted in college classes, and this, too, imposes new responsibilities on the college teacher.

Moreover, the increasing demands of the subject matter that we teach require more effective tools for helping students learn. Many academics find it easy to fall into nostalgia for an imagined golden age when no special effort was supposedly required to share the wisdom of one's discipline with well-prepared students. But setting aside the historical question of whether such a world ever existed or the moral and political questions about who was excluded from this academic Eden, such idealizations of the past ignore the fact that from literary criticism to biochemistry the subjects that we seek to share with students are much more demanding than they were a half century ago. Even if the student body had remained constant, much more effective approaches to teaching would be required.

Thus, higher education is faced with the problem of introducing ever more complex subjects to larger numbers of students who desperately need this knowledge but who are no longer part of a preeducated elite that can absorb that knowledge with relatively little effort. It is not surprising, therefore, that there have been widespread calls to reevaluate approaches to teaching and learning that have been passed down through generations of teachers and students without much serious evaluation.

There has been some backlash against these calls for a revolution in academic teaching in the form of the kind of pedagogical fundamentalism, as captured in Patrick Allitt's aggressively titled *I'm the Teacher, You're the Student* (2005), and large segments of higher education have simply ignored these new demands for greater pedagogical responsibility. Yet increasingly, instructors, academic leaders, and powerful stakeholders outside higher education are convinced that college teachers have an obligation to assure that as many of their students as possible master their disciplines.

Considerable progress has, in fact, been made in developing new resources with which to respond to these challenges. After three decades of tireless work in schools of education, at university teaching centers, and within most academic disciplines, we have at our disposal the most impressive set of pedagogical strategies and theories of learning ever assembled. Moreover, despite frequent attacks on the professoriat, there is also evidence that college instructors are becoming more serious about fulfilling their responsibilities as instructors. (See, for example, Beyer, Taylor, and Gillmore 2013; see also Alan and Jeanne Booth's Historians on Teaching website, http://www.historiansonteaching.tv/.) A network of teaching centers and professional organizations serves to spread new ideas about instruction throughout institutions of higher education across the globe. And the scholarship of teaching and learning has made great strides in convincing a significant portion of academia that instructors can approach problems in the classroom with the same intellectual intensity that they bring to their traditional research.

But the very richness and variety of these new strategies for increasing learning can be a source of confusion for contemporary instructors. Faced with choices among collaborative learning, active learning, problem-based learning, Just-in-Time Teaching, and the like, typical college teachers, who are not apt to have any training in pedagogical theory, may feel overwhelmed. They are apt to grab the strategy du jour and attempt to apply it, whether or not it is appropriate for the learning challenges at hand.

What is needed, therefore, is an approach that will provide instructors with a coherent strategy for bringing their teaching in line with the learning needs of their students. They must have a method for determining what students need to be able to do to succeed in their disciplines, and a scheme for helping them master these mental operations. They must have a means to overcome emotional obstacles to learning, criteria for determining which pedagogical tools are most appropriate in particular situations, and a plan for assessing the degree of student mastery of each element in this process. After two decades of work with instructors on four continents, it is increasingly clear that the Decoding the Disciplines approach can provide such a framework for responding to the challenge of increasing student learning.

To understand the potential impact of this approach, let us imagine a classroom in which the response to learning difficulties is very different from the one described at the beginning of this introduction. In the earlier class, the failure of students to learn was explained in terms of the inadequacies of the instructor or the students, and the case was closed. In our new class, like the previous one, students arrive with incomplete or even dysfunctional notions of what works in the discipline and the instructor's initial teaching strategies have limited success. But in this course the orientation toward learning problems is entirely different. In this second class these difficulties are the trigger for a systematic exploration of obstacles to learning in the discipline and of the kinds of mental operations that students must master to overcome such obstacles. These ways of operating are then explained and modeled for students, who are given opportunities to practice these skills and receive feedback, and potential emotional obstacles to learning are considered and dealt with. Student mastery of the core ways of operating is evaluated, and this information is used to fine-tune the process. Finally, this experiment in teaching and learning is shared with a larger community. Throughout, the instructor has a sense of direction and purpose, and students work in a learning environment that is rationally organized and understandable.

In our work with hundreds of instructors in many fields we have seen that Decoding the Disciplines can produce this kind of breakthrough in overcoming obstacles to learning. In decoded classes we have observed the emergence of new energy in students and faculty alike, and we have seen glimmers of new possibilities for using decoding as the basis for broader reforms of higher education and beyond.

The Development of Decoding the Disciplines

Decoding the Disciplines evolved over a dozen years as part of a faculty development program at Indiana University (IU), the Freshman Learning Project (FLP), which Joan Middendorf and I directed. The FLP began with the notion that student learning would increase if instructors were brought together to systematically explore ways to define and model the basic ways of thinking in their fields. From 1998 to 2010 a dozen faculty fellows from across the disciplines were identified each year on the basis of their involvement with student learning and the likelihood that the strategies they developed would have an impact on their colleagues. These instructors were invited to participate in an intensive two-week seminar in which they worked to devise new ways to help more students master particularly difficult skills in a course.

The FLP fellows concentrated on specific learning challenges in their individual disciplines, but within the intensely collaborative environment of the summer seminars and the planning sessions that preceded them a larger meta-strategy for increasing student learning evolved. The resulting process, which we named Decoding the Disciplines, provides a framework that facilitates serious thinking about the difficulties students face in a particular field and about strategies to help them overcome these challenges.

At the core of decoding lie three assumptions. The first is that all learning is local. Rather than trying to deal with something large and global, like critical thinking, we concentrate on learning in specific disciplines. After extensive analysis we may find that at a deeper level there are similar ways of thinking in two different disciplines, but we always begin by focusing on the particular forms of operating within a field.[1]

Second, we concentrate on what students have to *do*, not what they have to *know*. Content and concepts are, of course, important, but in the effort to increase student learning it is almost always more productive to focus on the mental operations that students must perform to succeed. Knowing always involves some kind of doing, and we are convinced that it is here that we can make a real difference in student learning.

Third, we assume that it is in the nature of expertise that many of the operations necessary to perform basic tasks in a field may not automatically be consciously evident to the specialist. As one moves through successively more difficult levels of learning in a discipline, it is necessary that many of the basic operations become so automatic that they are invisible to the person performing them. Systematic observations of many instructors have supported this assumption, and we have seen repeatedly that this naturally leads instructors to skip key steps when they try to convey the essence of their field. From the students' perspective, it is as if they are being provided with a series of instructions intended to guide them to a geographical location but that parts of these instructions have randomly been omitted. Those students with a particularly good sense of direction or who are already somewhat familiar with the terrain may find their way, but many who find the subject more demanding or lack previous training will be hopelessly lost.

These three operating principles—the centrality of disciplines, the focus on what students must do, and the realization that many of the most essential steps in most college courses may be invisible to experts in the field—established the foundation for a new framework for thinking about increasing student learning. Through interactions with the faculty fellows of the FLP, who made an enormous contribution to the development of decoding, we embedded these principles in a seven-step process that can guide instructors in identifying problem areas, define the crucial mental operations students needed to master, model these ways of operating for students, provide opportunities for practice and feedback, deal with motivational obstacles to learning, assess the mastery of key skills, and share the results.

It is very important that these steps be seen as a general framework for addressing learning problems and not as a rigid agenda for all teaching. There is a logic to the sequence, but there are situations in which the order might vary or only some of the steps might be fully implemented. If, for example, one were operating within a backward-design framework (Wiggins and McTighe 1998), it might be better to move from step 2 (defining operations) to step 6 (developing strategies for assessment) before thinking about steps 3 (modeling), 4 (practice and feedback), and 5 (emotional and motivational issues). It may sometimes be

THE SEVEN STEPS OF DECODING

Step 1: Identify a bottleneck. Identify a place in a course where many students encounter obstacles to mastering the material.

Step 2: Define the mental operations needed to get past the bottleneck. Explore in depth the steps that an expert in the field would go through to accomplish the tasks identified as a bottleneck. (This initially involved an intensive interview of the instructor by individuals outside that discipline, but alternative procedures have been developed for times when that is not optimal.)

Step 3: Model these tasks explicitly. Let the students observe the instructor going through the steps that an expert would complete to accomplish these tasks. Typically, this would involve the following actions:

- Provide a metaphor or analogy for the desired thinking.
- Perform the desired thinking in front of students with a disciplinary example.
- Explicitly highlight crucial operations in the example.
- Assure that this modeling is reinforced repeatedly by making it a part of the very architecture of the course.

Step 4: Give students practice and feedback. Construct assignments, team activities, and other learning exercises that allow students to do each of the basic tasks defined above and get feedback on their mastery of that skill.

Step 5: Motivate the students and deal with potential emotional blocks. Decide which approaches encourage students to excel and then utilize them to create an environment that fosters a positive learning environment. Identify any emotional bottlenecks to learning and work to help students reframe these issues.

Step 6: Assess how well students are mastering the mental operations. Create forms of assessment that provide specific information about the extent of student mastery of the particular learning tasks defined in step 2.

Step 7: Share what you have learned about your students' learning. Share what is being learned informally with colleagues or more formally in articles and presentations on the scholarship of teaching and learning. Consider the implications of this process in larger institutional contexts.

necessary to postpone step 7 (sharing) or the consideration of step 5 (emotional obstacles), or to spend a particular semester defining the necessary operations and modeling them without proceeding to the other steps until later. But regardless of the manner in which the paradigm is implemented, it is crucial that attention be paid to defining the basic operations that students must master to succeed in the course.

Going Through the Decoding Steps: An Example from a History Course

The description of the decoding steps presented above may seem somewhat abstract and removed from the practical realities of the classroom. In this section I will therefore share the process of using decoding in one of my own courses. Of necessity, the description contains a great deal of detail about the challenges and strategies involved in this particular experiment in teaching. The purpose of including this material is to highlight the process of strategic decision making that underlies decoding. The specific steps that were taken may be of little or no relevance to most disciplines outside history, but they will hopefully provide a clearer picture of how the power of the decoding paradigm can be brought to bear on the challenges the emerge in a particular course.

The Context

The context in which this project occurred was a little unusual: a full academic course taught in only nine days to fifteen students in the Indiana University Intensive Freshman Seminars program immediately before the start of their first semester. The students were entering college with a wide variety of intended majors and a level of skills that was slightly higher than average for the university. There were fewer distractions than in a normal semester, and I had their time from 9:00 to 5:30 each day. These assets were offset, however, by the challenge of introducing students who were new to college to unfamiliar ways of thinking and to a semester's worth of content in a very short period of time.

Step 1: Identify a Bottleneck

Decoding the Disciplines generally begins with the identification of an obstacle that is blocking the learning of significant numbers of students. In previous iterations of this course I had had some success at developing strategies for introducing students to many of the central mental operations needed in history courses, (Díaz, Middendorf, Pace, and Shopkow 2008; Pace 2004, 2012), but some basic skills still eluded some of the students. I could now, for example, successfully introduce them to the process of reading historically and using evidence to defend an argument. But a significant portion of the students typically taking the course still had difficulty generating their own interpretations of the issues being studied. When I gave them a thesis, they could support it with relevant evidence, but many of them could not independently move beyond the details to generate a coherent argument of their own. When faced with the challenge of writing a paper, they would quickly review the information that they have collected from the readings, lectures, and discussions, organize it into paragraphs that were generally arranged in the order in which the material was covered in the course, and then append at the beginning and the end vague generalizations about how things changed. At their worst the rhetorical structure of these essays sometimes resembled the high school history papers described by Kathleen McCarty Young and Gaea Leinhardt (1998) in which a succession of paragraphs took the form of a list without a central organizing principle. All of this convinced me that the students' difficulty in generating effective interpretations of historical phenomena was a bottleneck to learning that needed to be addressed in the next iteration of the decoding process.

Step 2: Define the Mental Operations Needed to Get Past the Bottleneck

In order to teach students to move from listing details to generating unifying interpretations, I needed to make explicit what professional historians do that is not just repeating dates and facts and to systematically teach these mental operations to my students. This raised the very thorny question of just how historians themselves generate arguments. For generations history instructors have written "Thesis?" on student papers that were not clearly organized around a central interpretation. But it is often not entirely clear, even to professionals in the field, exactly how this process is actually carried out. When the expert carefully processes historical documents, patterns seem to emerge magically from careful reading, and these congeal into interpretations. But "Use magic" is an inadequate instruction to students. It was therefore necessary to make conscious the steps that historians perform to turn isolated aspects of a phenomenon into a coherent argument.

Here I was clearly in step 2 of the decoding process, as I sought to define the mental operations that experts in the field automatically employ to generate theses. This is a step that can be very demanding intellectually because it requires making mental operations explicit that are so automatic to the professional that they have become invisible. As we shall see in chapter 2, this process involves a systematic exploration of the disciplinary unconscious and often requires the assistance of others outside the field. In this case, however, the process was greatly assisted by the prior work of Indiana University's History Learning Project (HLP), whose interviews with historians had already revealed a number of the things that historians do when they are moving from sources to interpretations. Since it is generally important in decoding to focus on teaching one mental operation at a time, I decided to focus my efforts on one skill that seemed to be particularly important: posing relevant questions about the phenomenon being studied.

Unlike many students, who rush to find an answer to a question without stopping to systematically interrogate the topic and the evidence at hand, professional historians carefully—if often unconsciously—consider a series of questions that help them move toward a greater understanding of the phenomenon at hand. They ask how a text or artifact was created. What interests, assumptions, or values shaped the decisions of its creators? How was it viewed by different groups in the population? How is it similar to or different from phenomena in other periods, other nations, or other aspects of the same culture? What is its significance in terms of the power relations, definitions of gender, and class structure of the time?

Questions like these are at the heart of all historical inquiry, but this questioning process seems so obvious to professional historians that it is rarely taught in history courses. Many students are unaware of the very need to interrogate elements of the past, and, even if they understand that this step is necessary, they may be ignorant of the kinds of questions that might lead them to an original interpretation.

Helping students master historical questioning also went straight to the core of a central epistemological misunderstanding that many students bring to college history courses. When students view history as a matter of collecting and organizing isolated dates and facts, it is quite natural for them to assume that their task is to memorize these details and to repeat back to the instructor the story they have been given about how these particular elements fit together. Thus, when assigned a paper, such students conceptualize their task as executing a "data dump" that demonstrates their knowledge of details (Shopkow et al. 2013a; Wineburg 2001). When they bring these notions of the discipline into a course in which they are asked to evaluate evidence, weigh competing interpretations, and reconstruct the perspectives of different historical actors, the results can be quite negative. If, however, their dysfunctional views of historical processing were replaced with a new emphasis on posing and answering questions, it might reshape their view of the field in ways that would also be very productive for other aspects of the course. Asking questions could, thus, reinforce other skills that I was already trying to instill in my students.

Step 3: Model the Required Mental Operations

The process of defining a crucial mental operation that students must master to overcome the bottleneck leads directly to the third step of the decoding process—modeling these operations for students. In this case it was necessary to make students aware of the need to stop and ask questions when exploring a historical phenomenon and to give them an idea of the kinds of questions that they might ask.

To give them a clear picture of how this looked in practice and to model the kinds of questions that might be posed, I showed them a short video in which one

IN-CLASS POWERPOINT SLIDE MODELING
THE PROCESS OF POSING QUESTIONS
TO ANSWER A QUESTION

Large Question to be Answered	*Smaller Questions to Help Find an Answer*
The official artistic establishment in France in the middle of the nineteenth century was living in the midst of rapid change, and yet they steadfastly focused all of their attention on trying to maintain tradition. Why?	• What role might tradition play in any society? • What might someone get out of trying to replicate the past? • What were the official "academic" painters of the mid-nineteenth century trying to do? What were their goals? How did they define great art? • What are some good examples of official French art in this period that seem to have been motivated by the desire to maintain tradition? • What did artists in France explicitly say about tradition? • When artists in this period thought about tradition, what did it look like to them? • What are some good examples of previous work that they would have wanted to imitate? • In what ways did the systems for producing, selling, and consuming art encourage the dominance of tradition and discourage innovation?

of the historians we interviewed described the kinds of questions that he would pose if he were trying to use the famous poster of Rosie the Riveter for understanding the American home front during World War II. This example came from outside the subject matter of the course, so we could discuss the general nature of the questions that the historian had asked and, more broadly, the role of questions in historical analysis (step 3, modeling) without the students assuming that their goal was simply to memorize these particular examples.

A single modeling exercise was, however, not enough to produce the kinds of deep mental changes that I was hoping for. Therefore, I returned to the modeling process repeatedly throughout the course. On the second day, for example. I showed them the kind of essay question that might have traditionally been asked in a course on our subject matter, and then I presented some of the smaller questions I might consider, if I were actually trying to develop an interpretation to response to the prompt.

Step 4: Give Students Practice and Feedback

On one plane the purpose of all this modeling was to give students some practical tools that would help them generate historical interpretations. But on a deeper level it was also intended to weaken the grip of a fact-and-date approach to history. To achieve this kind of transformation, students had to not only hear about these ways of processing the past, but also to have extensive experience at posing historical questions themselves.

Therefore, I created a structure for the course which would make posing questions a natural and automatic process for the students. Each day, after a period of traditional discussion and short lectures on the topic for the day, each of the four learning teams was given a different question to answer. Each student explored a set of potentially relevant sources and wrote an individual research report considering the ways in which this material might be used to answer the question at hand. Each team then had several hours to use these research reports as the basis for a presentation to the entire class at the end of the day; these presentations were then critiqued as if they were outlines for papers. In all of these activities and in the in-class exercises and the final paper, students were pressed to make explicit the questions that they were asking, as they inhabited a space in which posing historical questions became naturalized.

Step 5: Motivate the Students and Deal with Potential Emotional Blocks

As we shall see in chapter 5, the emotional side of learning has to be considered in decoding, just like its cognitive counterparts. This obviously requires motivating students to engage in the course work. But it is also important to anticipate and to counter any tendency of the students to reject the course because the nature of the work or the subject matter does not match their preconceptions of what is supposed to happen.

The format of the course I was teaching supported motivation through frequent shifts to different tasks across the day, which helped keep students focused. There was also something potentially empowering about the process, since the students were repeatedly asked to make choices and to become experts on small parts of the daily topic. Even more important was the fact that the process assured that students' work would be observed and evaluated by their peers, not just by the instructor. If they did not fully commit to the individual research each day, the shoddy work would be visible not only to me but also to their teammates who were depending on this contribution to the shared afternoon project. Again, at the end of the day the presentation and critique of each team's response to the question that had been posed for them was a shared experience, and it was very clear that none of the teams wanted to appear unprepared in front of its peers.

Yet, such motivational factors could have been overwhelmed if the students' preconceptions about what should occur in the course clashed with what I had planned for them. In this particular course there was relatively little in the content of the course that would be apt to evoke resistance from the students. But many of them brought to college preconceptions about the nature of history that were potentially in conflict with what they would experience in my class. At the first meeting of the class I talked about the ways in which the memorization of details, which many of them identified with history, was not very functional in the era of the internet and suggested that it would be much more useful in this course and beyond to develop their skill at posing relevant questions. But, the experience of history as memorization and repetition that had been automatic in some of their high school history classes might have still seemed safe and reassuringly familiar in a way that an emphasis on questioning and interpretation in my course did not. If the demands of my course had seemed completely overwhelming, there would remain the possibility that students would retreat into a belief that "real" history was about facts and dates.

Therefore, from the moment that the students received the first packet of information about the course, I needed to help them develop a sense that they could survive and even prosper in the kind of intellectual environment that I had created for them. The very structure of the course helped to minimize students' fear that they needed to remain in the realm of memorization to stay safe. The process through which the course had been created automatically broke large, amorphous tasks up into their constituent parts, and the mental operations necessary for successfully completing each of them were being carefully modeled. Their tasks were defined clearly, they could see their own progress and that of their fellow students, and, when they were confused about just what they needed to do, they were provided them with frequent opportunities to get help from me, the student intern, and their classmates. In such a world it was much more likely that students would respond positively to the notion that playing with evidence and generating interpretations was not only more useful in the long run, but that it was much more fun than laborious memorization.

Step 6: Assess How Well Students Are Mastering the Mental Operations

Step 6, assessing learning, flowed naturally from the structure of the course. The daily team presentations provided evidence about how effective the groups were at posing questions and producing interpretations, and they provided an occasion for feedback. The individual homework assignments provided more information about the extent to which particular students had mastered these skills. The students each produced a final paper complete with a list of the questions that they had posed to help them produce an interpretation, and these provided more information about the extent to which they were mastering the basic mental operations required in the course. And short pre- and posttests provided more information about changes in students' understanding of what it meant to apply historical reasoning.

Step 7: Share What You Have Learned about Your Students' Learning

The ideas that inspired this decoding endeavor emerged from a community of scholars of teaching and learning, and I am passing on that gift in the act of writing this.

Commentary

An attentive reader might note that there has been almost no mention of content in this description of the course. This is not because it is unimportant. The course dealt with Parisian culture and society from 1850 to 1900, a topic that is filled with important historical issues that I wanted my students to grapple with. But it was obvious from the beginning that, if I did not bring them into the world of historical reasoning, their encounter with the issues I cared about would be irrelevant. Students who assumed that the essence of the course was memorizing the date of the coup that led to Napoleon III becoming emperor would not be likely to really engage with the emergence of a modern consumer culture in Parisian department stores or the replacement of traditional, authoritarian art institutions with profit-based private galleries.

At every turn the steps needed to model basic processes of the historian's approach were embedded in material about the period under examination. The modeling process almost always involved specific developments in Paris in the late nineteenth century, and the practice required students to engage with primary and secondary sources linked to this era. Thus, content had a very important role in the course, even if it was not allowed to dominate all pedagogical decisions. And by the end of the course the students' grasp of the details of French history, as revealed in their final papers, was significantly more sophisticated than that of students in earlier pre-decoding versions of the course. Ironically, it turns out that students actually learn the facts of history better when they are actively putting them to use rather than focusing on trying to memorize them.

It is important, however, to close this little classroom short story with a reminder that the point here is not to copy the format of this particular course. Decoding made it easier for me to develop specific strategies to help more students overcome certain bottlenecks to learning, but the application of the paradigm to a different teaching challenge might produce radically different approaches. Decoding is not a technique that can simply be picked up and applied in a number of different contexts. Instead, it is a framework in which one can make clear and conscious strategic choices about choosing or inventing techniques that are particularly appropriate for the situation at hand. One might visit two decoded classes in which the activities were quite different, but beneath these differences there would be a common commitment to define and to remain focused on helping students master those specific mental operations that are needed to overcome existing bottlenecks.

Decoding as a Research Strategy

The Freshman Learning Project was designed as a relatively straightforward faculty development program aimed at developing and spreading ideas about teaching and learning within the local community at Indiana University–Bloomington. But the decoding process rapidly spread beyond those limits. Many of the faculty fellows from the FLP found that their projects could easily be transformed into the scholarship of teaching and learning, and they began to present papers and publish articles on this work. Joan Middendorf and I edited an issue of *New Directions in Teaching and Learning* in which the basics of decoding were presented and participants in the FLP shared their experiments with this paradigm (Pace and Middendorf 2004). This publication and a series of articles and presentations spread the paradigm widely, and groups around the world began applying this model and exploring its possibilities.

Joan played a crucial role in this process by organizing groups of instructors into research groups that applied the paradigm to particular problems, such as visual learning, emotional bottlenecks, and teaching students about diversity. But the real breakthrough occurred in 2006, when historians Leah Shopkow and Arlene Díaz joined Joan and me to form the History Learning Project. As was noted earlier in this chapter, the HLP videotaped interviews in which twenty-four historians were pressed to make explicit the mental operations they used to perform tasks that were daunting for many students in their courses. As the team expanded to include four faculty fellows and two PhD candidate fellows, we began to systematically model and assess many of these operations in history courses. And to provide a point of comparison with another discipline, we conducted a series of decoding interviews with geology faculty in which we explored the mental operations required for success in their field and compared them with those in history.

This work deepened Decoding the Disciplines. Arlene Díaz helped us develop more effective strategies for assessing learning in decoded courses and for using the paradigm beyond individual classrooms. Leah Shopkow helped us fully realize the ways in which most bottlenecks to learning are linked to students' misunderstanding of the basic epistemology of the disciplines they are studying. As a group, we gained increasing sophistication in our efforts to help instructors make explicit the basic mental operations their students must master. More effective strategies for modeling, practicing, and assessing these operations were developed, and an ever increasing emphasis was placed on the emotional obstacles that often stand in the ways of student learning. In the process, decoding was transformed into a tool for conducting systematic projects in the scholarship of teaching and learning.

Research groups in at least ten countries are now producing new approaches to each of the seven steps of the process. At institutions like Mount Royal University in Canada, the University of Bielefeld and the Ostfalia University of Applied Sciences in Germany, the University of Liège in Belgium, the University of the Free State in South Africa, University College Dublin in Ireland, Elon University in the United States, and a consortium of universities in Australia, scholars of teaching and learning are working with the paradigm and expanding its scope. The enthusiastic response that we have received from instructors and educational developers around the world and their request for more information has convinced us that it is time to make this approach available to a wider audience. As noted in the preface, in addition to the volume that you are reading, the HLP is completing work on a monograph that will show how decoding can transform teaching in a single discipline, and Joan Middendorf and Leah Shopkow are writing a practical guide to taking instructors through the seven steps (*Decoding the Disciplines,* forthcoming). A group at Mount Royal University in Calgary led by Janice Miller-Young and Jennifer Boman is sharing its work in *Using the Decoding the Disciplines Framework for Learning across Disciplines,* to be published in the *New Directions for Teaching and Learning* series, and there will undoubtedly be more studies on decoding in the future.

In the present volume, chapters 1–7 explore each of the seven steps of the decoding process; they are designed to be of use to instructors who are looking for a framework within which to increase learning and to scholars of teaching and learning who are seeking a model for their research. Suggestions will also be provided for the use of decoding on an institutional level by educational developers, by academic units seeking to rationalize their curriculum, and by university administrators seeking to assess learning and to represent the value of higher education to a broader public. Chapter 8 will consider future directions for this pedagogical paradigm.

Our experience working with instructors from a wide range of disciplines and institutions has convinced us that decoding can provide a framework within which faculty, educational developers, administrators, and scholars of teaching and learning can work productively to increase student learning both within individual courses and more broadly. Decoding is certainly not a technocratic solution to all educational problems, and it certainly does not replace all the ideas on teaching and learning that have emerged in recent decades. We still have to be concerned about questions of students' self-actualization, instructors' authenticity, and the personal interactions of student and teacher. And in many situations we cannot ignore the broader cultural, economic, and social context within which students learn or the impact of gender, race, class, sexual orientation, or other forms of identity.

But it is also true that no amount of attention to individual, relational, or social factors will produce great increases in learning if courses remain chaotic places in which crucial steps are unintentionally hidden from students and the path to success is littered with traps that threaten to end all progress. Decoding provides a process for systematically analyzing and minimizing the difficulties that prevent so many students from realizing their potential. It can allow us to make more effective use of the abundance of teaching techniques that are now available, and it can provide more students with access to the wisdom that lies buried deep in the core of all disciplines.

It is important to stress once again the collaborative nature of this work. All the progress that has been attained to date has been the result of instructors and educational developers building on the work of others and readapting the model to fit their own needs and concerns. Hopefully this process will continue into the future. Because decoding is not an orthodoxy to be slavishly followed, it is assumed that, as this work spreads, the appropriation and adaptation of the paradigm in different contexts will take it in directions that its creators can never anticipate. Or to put it contemporary terms, this system is intended to be Linux, not Microsoft.

Thus, we welcome readers to the decoding community. From its inception the experience of working with others on this paradigm and sharing its benefits with students has been one of the richest professional and personal experiences of my life. I have been blessed at every stage of this process with generous and insightful colleagues—particularly Arlene Díaz, Joan Middendorf, and Leah Shopkow—who have contributed enormously to the development of this approach. I hope that you will find participation in the decoding community equally rewarding.

Decoding and Instructors' Experience

As the previous description must make clear, creating a course that really focuses on helping more students to overcome common bottlenecks requires a good deal more up-front planning. While this often serves to minimize instructor's frustration and conflict and can actually make some traditional aspects of teaching, such as grading, less onerous, college instructors may be forgiven for a certain skepticism when confronted with a new framework for thinking about teaching and learning in their courses. There is little evidence that the typical college teacher has a great deal of extra time to dabble in pedagogical experimentation. To the contrary, as Pat Hutchings, Mary Huber, and Tony Ciccone have put it quite clearly, the pressures on college instructors have increased enormously; they note that

> It is hard not to be struck by the escalating demands on faculty today. Even as serious intellectual work on learning and teaching has begun to make a place for itself in campus culture, so have pressures in other directions: rising expectations, even in so-called teaching institutions, for traditional research publications; urgings in the direction of more interdisciplinary scholarship; growing commitments to community engagement; new opportunities but also new challenges in the use of technology; high-profile imperatives around assessment, accountability, student recruitment, retention, and advising; and— most to the point here—an increasingly urgent public call to move much larger numbers of students toward more meaningful forms and levels of learning. (Hutchings, Huber, and Ciccone 2011, 10)

Instructors, living in the midst of a maelstrom of personal and professional pressures, might thus feel a certain skepticism about new schemes for restructuring a major part of their professional life. These doubts would understandably increase if they were asked to learn an entirely new disciplinary language, to completely uproot everything that they had already created in their courses, or to submit to a process that was being imposed on them by those higher up in the academic food chain. Fortunately, decoding does none of these things. It is always centered on instructors' own learning goals and is couched in a language that is familiar to those in the field. It focuses on a particular area that instructors themselves have identified as problematic, and changes remain linked to solving that particular problem rather than seeking to re-create a course from scratch. Instead of asking instructors to pick sides in a battle of competing pedagogical theories, it provides criteria for selecting the approaches that are most appropriate for particular learning situations. It is always faculty directed and, while it may eventually have a much broader impact, it always begins as a response to problems in specific courses.

Nonetheless, if there were not significant personal advantages for instructors in undertaking decoding, it might be a hard sell. Fortunately, there are some very powerful benefits to be gained. Perhaps, most important, is the sense of empowerment that decoding often brings. In the past far too many college teachers have found themselves powerless to bring about meaningful learning in their courses. They begin their careers desperately wanting to share the gift of their discipline with students, but they find that a chasm exists between their notion of what needs to be done in the field and the work that their students turn in. They soon exhaust the tools available to them and settle in for a career of frustration, having no way to feel good about a central element of their professional life except to displace their negative feelings onto their students.

Decoding provides instructors with a means to break out of this cycle of frustration and failure by applying the reasoning power that they have developed in their traditional disciplinary research to practical challenges in the classroom. It offers them not a prepackaged, top-down solution to learning problems but instead a framework within which to solve these problems themselves. It is a compass, not an itinerary. It gives instructors a means of orienting themselves in the midst of the potentially confusing landscape of the classroom, but they will ultimately determine which direction they will take. And by enabling them to identify a particular obstacle to learning and to systematically work to minimize its impact on students, decoding allows instructors to create for themselves a new sense of direction and power in a crucial area of their professional life.

The potential impact of this approach was captured by Janice Miller-Young and Jennifer Boman in their description of the experience of instructors in a wide range of disciplines at Mount Royal University:

> The advantage of the Decoding the Disciplines model is its engagement of the practitioner. We know that traditional research on pedagogy and novice-expert differences will not necessarily convince faculty members to change their teaching practice . . . In our study most participants, at some point in their interview, articulated a sudden and unprompted realization that describing their own thinking process or describing a personal experience that was influential to their own learning might be helpful for their students. . . . [O]ur observations described above suggest that using the Decoding model has a potentially transformative effect on faculty's teaching practice. . . . For these reasons we suggest that the Decoding model holds much promise for a variety of faculty development initiatives as well as a method for pedagogical research. (Miller-Young and Boman, "Uncovering," forthcoming)

1. FINDING THE BOTTLENECK

The Strategic Importance of Bottlenecks

Teaching is, of necessity, a strategic undertaking. Time and resources are limited; they must be focused with precision and skill. To be effective, teachers need to know where and when to intervene. They must have at their disposal an array of effective teaching techniques, but they also need a broad framework to determine which interventions will produce the maximum effect on learning in a particular situation.

Decoding the Disciplines provides such a strategic framework. It offers a context for decision making within which instructors, educational developers, and college administrators can determine the most appropriate course of action. Decoding is not in itself a teaching technique, but instead a framework within which to decide which techniques are most appropriate at a particular moment. As such, it provides a means for taking full advantage of the flowering of pedagogical thinking that has occurred in the last thirty years.

At the core of Decoding is the concept of the *bottleneck*. In fields such as engineering and computer science, the restriction of the flow of liquid at the neck of a bottle has been used as a metaphor for those places in a complex system where performance is most apt to be restricted. In the context of the scholarship of teaching and learning, the term indicates those places in a course where the stream of learning is particularly apt to be obstructed. While students may move easily through parts of a course, there can be other places where large numbers of them encounter obstacles to learning that they find very difficult to overcome. Being unable to master a particular obstacle may not in itself immediately lead to failure, but as bottlenecks mount up, students become increasingly confused, less and less able to perform the basic tasks required in the course.

The decision to begin by looking at the places where students get stuck may seem so obvious that it does not need to be stated. But in fact, a great deal of the effort that is devoted to improving instruction ignores this crucial step. It is quite easy to become so enamored of a new teaching technique that one begins trying to apply it everywhere. As John Bransford and his colleagues have put it, "Asking which teaching technique is best is analogous to asking which tool is best—a hammer, a screwdriver, a knife, or pliers. In teaching as in carpentry, the selection of tools depends on the task at hand and the materials one is working with" (Bransford, Brown, and Cocking 2000, 22). The first step in the decoding process, therefore, focuses attention on the task, not on the tool box.

Beginning with bottlenecks has two other important functions. First, it serves as a counterweight to content. Academics love their subject matter, and the impulse to share it can easily overwhelm the intention to help students master basic skills. Learning problems, however, generally arise not from a lack of access to content but from students' inability to process that content once it has been obtained. Concentrating on bottlenecks keeps attention focused on what students have to be able to *do,* not what they have to remember.

Second, this approach narrows the instructor's field of vision in a productive manner. Faced with students who are not learning, we are often tempted to try to rush in and fix everything at once. Unfortunately, global efforts to change everything about a course are apt to be unfocused, and attempts to simultaneously instill all of the elements of critical thinking often confuse both the instructor and the student. Moreover, such complex goals are generally impossible to assess and refine because it is impossible to know which interventions are or are not working.

By contrast, the instructor using decoding operates like Adam Smith's celebrated pin manufacturer who discovered that, by breaking production up into its constituent parts, each aspect of the process could be analyzed and perfected. By concentrating on a particular bottleneck, an instructor is more able to identify the mental operations that are required for success in this area, to devise strategies to model these specific skills, to create opportunities for students to practice them, and to assess the ways in which these efforts do or do not help students overcome this obstacle to learning. As an added bonus, we have found that when students really master the steps needed to get past a bottleneck, they quite often gain a deeper understanding of the nature of the discipline that allows them to move past other potential impediments to learning on their own.

Bottlenecks and Threshold Concepts

This focus on bottlenecks to learning emerged from the rich conceptual stew that has been simmering in discussions about higher education since the 1980s and 1990s. The increased attention to critical thinking played a crucial role, by shifting focus from the transmission of information to the engendering of key mental processes in students (see, for example, Kurfiss 1988). This transformed the significance of student errors; learning problems that had often been dismissed as a consequence of students' cognitive deficits or unwillingness to work now came to be seen as the result of a failure to adequately introduce students to required ways of thinking. Similarly, the shift of focus from teaching to learning, described by Robert Barr and John Tagg in their influential article on the "learning paradigm" (1995), automatically set the stage for greater concern with those places where learning was not occurring.

At the same time, there was increased concern with learning in the disciplines.[1] It became clear that in the university context learning is almost always "local"—that is, it is conditioned by the specific epistemology and procedures of a particular academic sphere (Donald 2002; Pace and Middendorf 2004; Shulman 1986, 1993; Tobias 1992–93). As Lee Shulman put it in his description of pedagogical content knowledge, "if different disciplines value particular forms of evidence and argument, narrative, and explanation, then their pedagogies should reflect the same forms of representation and exposition" (2002, vii). The perceived need to make the emerging field of the scholarship of teaching and learning available to instructors in a broad range of fields also played a role in this new emphasis on disciplinary forms of knowledge. As Mary Taylor Huber and Sherwyn P. Morreale put it, "For good or for ill, scholars of teaching and learning must address field-specific issues if they are going to be heard in their own disciplines, and they must speak in a language that their colleagues understand" (2002, 2). This focus on the disciplinary conditions for learning was reinforced by the notion that learning should be viewed as a kind of apprenticeship in which students are drawn into the cognitive, practical, and ethical practices of a discipline (Brown, Collins, and Duguid 1989). Knowing, thus, came to be conceptualized within this approach as a form of doing, and this doing varied from field to field.

Within this flow of new ways of understanding learning, there emerged a sense that more attention needed to be paid to places where students get stuck. Starting in the late 1990s, educational theorists and scholars of teaching and learning began to develop theories of difficulty in which obstacles to learning were treated not as a problem to be swept away as quickly as possible but as an intellectual puzzle to be solved (Bass 1999). David Perkins's "troublesome knowledge" (1999, 2006), Jan Meyer and Ray Land's "Threshold concepts" (2003, 2006), and my and Joan Middendorf's Decoding the Disciplines process (Pace and Middendorf 2004) all developed during this period simultaneously, but independently, in the United Kingdom, Australia, and the United States.

The threshold concepts model is particularly relevant to those interested in decoding, and the relationship between the two approaches is worth exploring briefly. (Readers who are less interested in the theoretical underpinnings of these ways of thinking about learning should feel free to skip to the next section of this chapter.) Scholars focusing on threshold concepts have identified a number of essential ideas that are crucial to understanding particular disciplines. If such concepts are not mastered, students' further progress in the field is blocked. Such concepts are transformative (they involve a fundamental shift in a student's understanding of the subject), integrative (they reveal hidden connections), and probably irreversible (Meyer and Land, 2003, 2005, 2006; O'Mahony et al. 2014).

Those working within the threshold paradigm have emphasized the emotional costs that often accompany such intellectual transformations.

Decoding the Disciplines and threshold concepts are complementary approaches to understanding student difficulties, and practitioners of each model can benefit from the other. A more extended discussion of the relationship between the two approaches has been presented by Leah Shopkow (2010), whose work in this area has greatly influenced my own formulations. But at the core there are five essential differences between the two paradigms.

1. *The bottlenecks with which decoding begins occupy a larger conceptual territory than do threshold concepts.* As my colleague Joan Middendorf first recognized, threshold concepts are a subset of a larger territory of bottlenecks. Some bottlenecks do involve central issues in particular disciplines and can be considered threshold concepts, but others may arise from other issues. Decoding might consider obstacles to learning such as a student's inability to understand how to process feedback on exams or to move beyond the standard answers to a problem in order to generate alternative solutions. It also deals with emotional obstacles to learning (see chapter 6). Thus, while all threshold concepts are bottlenecks, all bottlenecks are not threshold concepts.

2. *Bottlenecks are not necessarily as transformative as threshold concepts.* Threshold concepts are conceptualized as central portals through which all students must pass to master a particular discipline. Students who successfully manage this difficult passage are transformed, and the process is irreversible. They will never again be able to think in the ways in which they did before this transformation. By contrast, some bottlenecks have these qualities, but others do not have such revolutionary consequences. It is necessary for students to get past them, but they are more like rough patches on a long trail than they are life-changing alterations to students' worldviews.

3. *As the word* concept *suggests, the search for threshold concepts generally centers on what students have to know, whereas decoding is much more concerned with what students have to do.* In some cases this is a subtle distinction, but it is an important one. Decoding consistently focuses on the mental operations that students must perform, not on the intellectual concepts that they must learn. Its goal is conceived in terms of verbs, not nouns.

4. *Threshold concepts generally begin with the knowledge of how a discipline works as it is consciously understood by experts in the field, whereas decoding problematizes the discovery of mental operations within a field.* Threshold concepts tend to focus on concepts, such as marginal utility in economics, whose importance is clear to virtually anyone in the discipline. Within decoding, by contrast, the crucial mental operations generally only become fully clear after a systematic process of exploration unearths crucial steps that may not have been conscious in the mind of the expert at the beginning

of the procedure (see chapter 2). This distinction is not absolute, but to understand the differences between the approaches, it is important to recognize that practitioners of threshold concepts will generally be working within the preexisting concepts of a discipline, whereas decoding may generate information about the nature of learning in the field that was not previously recognized. (For an extended discussion of this difference, see Shopkow 2010.)

5. *The concern with bottlenecks is only the first step in the decoding process, whereas those working within the threshold concept model must turn elsewhere for concrete steps to address the learning problem.* Decoding moves beyond the analysis of student difficulties to suggest a series of practical steps to help students overcome obstacles to learning, to assess the success of these interventions, and to share what has been learned with others. Thus, those working within the threshold concepts framework may choose to draw upon the later steps of decoding to address the learning problem at hand.

The two processes are complementary, and both have provided powerful ways of framing student difficulty that are potentially transformative for both the instructor and the students. Those working within the decoding paradigm can benefit from threshold concepts' focus on the learning that is most central to a discipline and on the emotional impact of such potentially wrenching intellectual and personal transformations. Conversely, the second step of the decoding process can make explicit hidden disciplinary ways of operating that would otherwise have been missed. This is particularly important in fields like the humanities, where there is generally less explicit consensus on key concepts and procedures. Moreover, decoding provides concrete strategies for helping students overcome obstacles to learning in any field.

The compatibility of decoding and threshold concepts has been demonstrated by Randy Bass and his colleagues, who created a faculty development program that merged the two approaches (Bass et al. 2011). In a subsequent article Kenneth Bain and Randy Bass refer to the "natural compatibility" between the two approaches and add that "this is a particularly rich marriage of the two approaches, primarily because threshold concept theory lacks a pedagogical design or faculty development elements; similarly, the instructional bottleneck approach [in decoding]—being strong in design and development—can break down intellectual activities into smaller manageable parts without losing sight of the more complex integrative picture" (2012, 200–201).

Defining Bottlenecks

The decoding process is usually more effective when the bottleneck is defined with some precision. The later steps of the process can lead to a sharpening of the understanding of the obstacle to learning, but it is still more efficient to make the initial statement of the problem as clear and distinct as possible. In formulating the bottleneck it is best to avoid disciplinary jargon and to define the issue in terms that would be understandable to any educated person. This not only makes the nature of the problem clear to those from other disciplines who can provide essential help in the subsequent steps, but it also makes it less likely that crucial elements of the process will remain hidden.

It is also better to define bottlenecks relatively narrowly. Thus, the commonly stated complaint of instructors that "students can't interpret texts" is so vague and general that it does not provide a particularly effective point of departure for an exercise in decoding. A more effective approach would be to formulate the problem less globally, as in, "Students want to go directly to interpreting a text without first getting a good grasp of a text's content. They need to observe before they interpret, but they are constantly skipping a thoughtful observation stage." With this beginning one could easily proceed to the later stages of decoding and define precisely what experts in the field do when they observe a text thoughtfully, and then to model this for students.

Here are a few of the bottlenecks that have been identified in the growing literature on decoding:

- *Political science.* Students often have difficulty recognizing the tension between majority rule and minority rights (Bernstein 2012).
- *Music history.* Many students have difficulty identifying the features that distinguish one musical style or genre from another (Burkholder 2011).
- *Law.* Students can be mesmerized by the sensational details of a case and miss the underlying legal principles (Somers 2014).
- *Criminal justice.* Students tend to view learning about research methods as an unnecessary part of their training (Sundt 2010).
- *Math education.* Students have difficulty developing a sequence of tasks used to teach a new concept (Schultz and Lovin 2011).
- *Journalism.* Students have difficulty generating story ideas (Haney 2015).

At some point we hope that a pedagogical Carl Linnaeus will emerge to generate a systematic typology of bottlenecks. This work is still too new, and too many "species" of mistakes remain uncataloged to complete that task at present. And, strategically, it was important to focus initially on the specific problems that emerge in particular disciplines. Nonetheless, certain patterns have emerged that appear in multiple fields. Here are a few of the areas in which students commonly have difficulty doing the kinds of work that are necessary for success:

- *Procedural problems.* In many fields students rush to find solutions before the nature of the challenge is sufficiently understood, or they fail to employ strategies in an appropriate order. In a math class, for example, students may not understand that there are points at which they need to stop and systematically consider a number of possible paths to follow in solving a problem.

- *Missing steps.* In other situations the difficulty arises because there are specific steps in the process of disciplinary work that students are not familiar with. For example, when students are presented with an artifact in a history course, they may not recognize it is necessary to compare it with artifacts produced in other cultures, other eras, or other social groups before they rush into trying to understand its significance.
- *Transferring processes.* Often the problem emerges because students do not know how to transfer a process from one context to another or even that such transfer is necessary. Physics students often encounter difficulties when they fail to understand the applicability of a physical principle to a problem in a different area.
- *Moving back and forth from models to concrete situations.* In some disciplines the process of connecting graphs or other models with concrete events can be problematic. In economics courses, for example, students often have difficulty relating abstract models to specific evidence.
- *Integration of details.* Learning problems can emerge when students do not understand how to move from the memorization of lists of facts to the integration of elements into a coherent whole. Art history students might create a list of characteristics of particular artists without ever grasping the unity of a particular style or genre.
- *Issues of scale.* Bottlenecks can also arise because students cannot adjust to thinking on scales that are very different from those they are accustomed to or cannot recognize that very different rules may apply for different scales. They may not know how to wrap their minds around the immensity of time and space that they encounter in courses in astronomy or geology, or the minuteness of subatomic particles. Or they may not understand that the laws of physics that apply on the level of everyday life are not applicable to interactions within the atom.
- *Procedures for knowledge generation.* More fundamentally, students may not understand how to generate knowledge within a field. If, for example, they imagine that a discipline like history or biology is based on the collection and memorization of simple "facts," they may not understand the necessity of generating coherent arguments supporting a systematic interpretation of these details.

Working with Bottlenecks

Making bottlenecks the first step in a systematic effort to increase learning requires an important shift on the part of instructors. Academics are often accustomed to think of the mistakes that students make simply as problems that need to be dealt with as rapidly as possible and then forgotten. Instead, we need to follow the lead of Randy Bass (1999), who in a seminal article on the scholarship of teaching and learning suggested that we need to consider the problems that emerge in the classroom in the same manner that we view the problems that we seek to solve in our research—that is, as opportunities for serious investigation. Following this line of reasoning, the mistakes that students make in our courses become gifts that can serve to increase our understanding of how to better teach our disciplines and can even illuminate the deeper nature of those disciplines.

Decoding generally begins with a consideration of where students are having the most difficulty in a course. These problem locations may jump immediately to mind, but sometimes it may require a more systematic reexamination of students' work. It is often worth creating situations in which students' mastery of certain procedures in a field—or the lack thereof—is made obvious. Early in a semester, for example, geologist Claudia Johnson asked her students to answer four questions about an academic paper they had been assigned:

1. What is the question presented by the authors?
2. What are the data they considered?
3. What are their interpretations of these data?
4. Are the authors adhering to their data in their interpretations?

When she read the students' answers, she found that most of them confused data, methods, and interpretations despite the fact that the paper had clear methods and data sections. She emerged from this experience with a new awareness that many of her students faced a bottleneck to learning that a professional geologist with years of experience in reading scholarly articles might never detect. Until they had a clearer notion of how experts in the field process a scholarly article, their progress would be limited.

Finding bottlenecks is rarely, if ever, a serious challenge to instructors. In fact, students are generally so generous in presenting us with obstacles to their learning that most experienced teachers can easily identify more bottlenecks than they will ever have time to investigate. Therefore we need to have strategic criteria for determining which offer the most promising occasions for interventions.

The simplest basis for deciding which bottlenecks to work on is to focus on those that are most apt to block students' further learning. In most cases, for example, a failure to use proper citation form is a less serious and less permanent obstacle to learning than an inability to perform some of the core operations of the discipline.[2] A bottleneck that only appears in one section of a single course and does not interfere with learning in other aspects of the field would be a less pressing candidate for decoding than one that is ubiquitous and central to many aspects of the discipline. Threshold concepts are particularly promising targets for decoding, but other problems such as difficulty in processing lectures or emotional resistance to the content of a course, may be more pressing in specific situations.

Instructors should also consider the distribution of the problem within the population of students typically enrolled in a particular course or sequence of courses. It is rare for a bottleneck to stop the learning of every student in a course. Therefore, it is necessary to make serious practical and ethical decisions about which problems are most in need of a response. If only one or two students are blocked at a particular point, it is sometimes necessary to focus one's attention on other obstacles to learning that are creating major problems for much larger numbers of students. In the long run it is to be hoped that preparatory courses, web resources, or outside tutoring will be made available to these students. As we shall see in chapters 7 and 8, the incorporation of decoding into curricular development and student advising can lessen the frequency of such mismatches between student abilities and the demands of a particular course. But in any particular semester it may be necessary to focus one's limited resources where it is needed by larger numbers of students.

Somewhat to our surprise, we have found that the emotional reaction of instructors to certain kinds of student errors often provides a useful criteria for determining which bottlenecks are most worthy of attention. The frustration that instructors feel when faced with certain kinds of bottlenecks has turned out to commonly be an indication that they are particularly worth addressing. We suspect that this is due to the fact that the most serious obstacles to learning generally arise from a fundamental misunderstanding of the epistemology of the discipline (see chapter 2). When an instructor is particularly bothered by mistakes, students are very often unintentionally operating according to procedures that violate the basic ways of creating knowledge in the field. Since the instructor is deeply immersed in such ways of knowing, mistakes of this nature seem particularly egregious. Thus, the emotional responses of instructors should be given serious consideration in deciding which bottlenecks to focus on.

To turn the bottleneck into an opportunity, however, it is essential to be sure that the identification of problem areas does not become the occasion for student bashing or vague cultural critiques. Faculty complaints that students do not make a serious commitment to the work in a particular course may be understandable, but this formulation of the problem is of little use if it leads only to nostalgia for an imaginary golden age of dedicated students or to random observations about the decline of culture in the modern world. As we shall see in chapter 5, motivational problems can be decoded, but only if they are examined with a certain detachment. Within the context of decoding a perception that some students don't care about one's discipline should lead directly to a systematic consideration of what causes experts in the field—or committed students—to take

---

CHARACTERISTICS OF USEFUL BOTTLENECKS

- They affect the learning of significant numbers of students.
- They interfere with major learning in a course or courses.
- They are defined clearly and without jargon.
- They are relatively focused and do not involve a large number of very disparate operations.

---

interest in the subject and of how these modes of operating could be engendered in more students.

Embracing the Bottleneck

Decoding the Disciplines, threshold concepts, and Perkins's "troublesome knowledge" all began with the notion that there are certain places in disciplines where significant numbers of students encounter obstacles to learning that can interrupt progress toward mastery of the field. These approaches can serve as a framework within which to increase student learning; as we have seen, they focus our attention on those places where student learning is most threatened and provide a starting point for effective intervention in the process.

But, like all perspectives, the focus on overcoming bottlenecks automatically predisposes those who adopt it to concentrate on certain possibilities and to ignore others. Until recently, I had devoted all my attention to helping students overcoming such obstacles as rapidly as possible and had failed to seriously consider whether the encounter with certain bottlenecks might sometimes be valuable in itself. Fortunately, I work within a broad community of scholars of teaching and learning who are constantly exploring new perspectives. Thus, I was exposed to a very different way of thinking about bottlenecks in comments by computer scientist Ali Erkan during a session at the Annual Meetings of the International Society for the Scholarship of Teaching and Learning in 2015, in which he suggested that bottlenecks can be viewed much more positively and strategically. His comments are worth quoting at length:

> When we reflect on our own education, we remember that some of the most important moments of learning had occurred when we tackled significant problems. Consequently, as educators, we try to inject similar challenges into our curriculum so that our students go through comparable experiences. But of the endless list of exercises and problems, which ones do we choose so that our curriculum gets stronger, the intellectual gain is maximized, and the frustration caused by non-intellectual aspects of the "struggle" is minimized? What challenges afford our students the greatest progress to becoming computer scientists? What accomplishments encourage them to own the learning process?
>
> Discussions on bottlenecks and threshold concepts typically have a reactionary tone to them because we are genuinely interested in helping our

students. But since particular forms of problems are deeply connected with progress, these two lenses [bottlenecks and threshold concepts] can also be used to guide a problem-selection process. This distinction is subtle but important: identifying the intellectual challenges of problems so that we can provide the right support when students need it, versus, knowing the state of our students and challenging them with "worthy" problems where "worth" is based on our understanding of bottlenecks and threshold concepts.... In other words, whether we use bottlenecks and threshold concepts as early warning mechanisms or as filters for picking the right challenge. (Erkan 2015)

Erkan's comments emphasize the importance of recognizing the value of students' experience of working through certain bottlenecks and the possibility of making informed, strategic decisions about how and when students encounter them. He is suggesting that the very difficulty of the bottleneck can make it a crucial part of the learning experience if it is used carefully and consciously.

Erkan describes a process through which students are intentionally presented with an apparent contradiction within the theoretical framework of computer science that can only be resolved by a fundamental conceptual shift. The encounter with this problem can be experienced by students as a bottleneck to learning, and we might be inclined to help students resolve the problem as quickly as possible. But Erkan emphasizes the positive potential in the student encounter with a problem that they cannot solve via their existing concepts. He views this challenge as a real learning opportunity to be sought out rather than simply overcome, and he carefully chooses the moment and the form in which this potential problem is confronted.

When we opt for such a strategic embrace of bottlenecks, we can gain greater control over students' encounters with potentially problematic intellectual transformations. To borrow a term from Thomas Kuhn, we can consciously decide when to allow students to continue operating within the context of "normal science" in which they are operating with existing and clearly defined intellectual contexts, and when to present them with a challenge that can only be surmounted with a paradigm shift. And we can prepare them for this moment by providing the intellectual scaffolding and emotional support that they need to successfully navigate these dangerous waters.

To take full advantage of the opportunity of bottlenecks, we can borrow Lev Vygotsky's concept of a zone of proximal development. Rejecting earlier psychologists' focus on what learning tasks students could perform on their own, Vygotsky considered the area in which students can engage in intellectual work with support but not independently. He defined this zone of proximal development as "the distance between the actual developmental level as determined by independent problem solving and the level of potential development as determined through problem solving under adult guidance or in collaboration with more capable peers" (1978, 86). He compared the mental operations in this zone to buds or flowers, as compared to the fruits of fully mastered skills, and it is in this area, he argued, that real learning takes place.

This notion can provide a framework within which to strategically situate students' encounters with key bottlenecks. If we only present students with problems that they can easily solve using existing mental operations, paradigmatic shifts in their understanding of the discipline are less likely to occur. If these challenges are completely beyond students' abilities, fundamental learning is not apt to occur, despite all of our efforts to the contrary. Such breakthroughs are, however, more likely to occur if we structure courses so that students encounter fundamental challenges at a moment when they have sufficient mastery of the field to be able to perform new operations within a supporting framework.

Of course, in practice, finding such a "sweet spot" for learning is not always easy. It can be difficult to predict when students will be in this zone of maximum learning, and different members of a class may reach it at very different times. Nonetheless, in a course that has been taught repeatedly, it may be possible to anticipate when such moments are apt to occur and thus to present bottlenecks that require paradigmatic shifts at the time when students are most able to be able to respond to the challenge. By proactively choosing the form and the timing of the encounter with the conceptual obstacle, the instructor can greatly increase the likelihood that students will be able to make crucial breakthroughs.

It is important to remember that those situations in which such experiences of struggle are in themselves productive are probably rare. Most bottlenecks are noise in the system, and the greater the ease with which students overcome them the better. Nonetheless, the process of orchestrating students' encounter with those bottlenecks that involve paradigmatic shifts can, as Erkan suggests, play an important role in aiding student mastery of a field.

From Bottlenecks to Mental Operations

If the process of identifying bottlenecks is taken seriously, it can be the beginning of a real transformation in the role of instructors. The failure of many students to accomplish the tasks given them in a college course can become an exciting intellectual challenge that redefines the role of the teacher and lessens the gap between the enterprises of teaching and research. Moreover, decoding's emphasis on the bottleneck keeps our eyes on the prize. It draws our attention to those areas in which actions are most needed.

However, identifying bottlenecks does not, in itself, solve the problem. It tells us where to concentrate our efforts, but not what we need to do to bring about real learning. To help students overcome this difficulty, we need to better understand what creates it in the first place. As we shall see in subsequent chapters, at the core of most bottlenecks is a mismatch between what students think they are supposed to do and what really brings success in a particular discipline. This generally results from a fundamental misunderstanding of knowledge formation in the field—its epistemology. Working from an inaccurate map of the discipline, students go astray. Our task, therefore, is to provide them with a better notion of what is actually required of them.

To accomplish this we need to set our mental maps of our discipline alongside students' conceptions of what is required to succeed in our courses. This will allow us to see more clearly what is missing in students' understanding of what needs to be done. Only then can we correct the misunderstandings and supply the missing pieces.

This requires us to have a very clear idea of what we ourselves do when functioning as experts in the discipline. Such an understanding might seem to be automatic in the professional who has been operating for years in a particular field, but as we shall see, the nature of expert knowledge can makes this seemingly simple task quite demanding. Thus, before we can fully show students what they must do to succeed in our courses, we must interrogate our own knowledge. This process constitutes the second step in the decoding process, and it will be the subject of chapter 2.

2. DECODING THE DISCIPLINARY UNCONSCIOUS

The Mystery of the Purloined Skills

The kinds of bottlenecks discussed in chapter 1 are so ubiquitous that we often treat them as facts of nature that need no explanation. We take it for granted that many students in our classes will have difficulties in learning, but we rarely stop to consider what causes these phenomena—beyond the usual complaints that students aren't trying, that they lack some innate ability necessary for work in our field, or that secondary schools are not doing their job. Such explanations may sometimes have an element of truth, but they accept as natural and inevitable the very thing that we are trying to prevent. To escape this trap we must transform student failure from a burden to be endured to a problem to be solved. And to accomplish this it is necessary to stop viewing student failure as a natural occurrence and view it as a phenomenon that requires examination.

At this very moment, students are sitting in classrooms around the world, unable to comprehend material that is being presented to them. Outside class these same human beings soak up information from their world like sponges. They have readily assimilated cultural systems that are so complex that outside anthropologists spend years trying to understand them. They have access to instructors who are highly expert in their subjects and who fervently wish for their students to succeed. And yet, for many of these students nothing meaningful is happening in the classroom. The instructor's words do not connect. They finish the course no more able to function in the field than when they arrived.

There are many historical, social, political, and economic factors that contribute to this strange mismatch between the learning potential of students and what happens in the classroom. These contributing factors have received some attention from scholars and need to be examined in much greater detail if we are to fully grapple with the challenges facing higher education. But for now our goal is to explore what instructors themselves can do to increase learning in the context within which they work. Therefore, we need to focus on why the words and actions of experts in the field are so often unintelligible to their students.

Let us begin the exploration of this phenomena with the consideration of a simple story. In the summer seminars of Indiana University's Freshman Learning Project (FLP) the program's faculty fellows were sent to courses in fields very different from their own to get a better sense of how courses differ across the curriculum. In one particular year the instructors from the humanities who visited a math class returned looking beaten and dispirited, while those from the sciences emerged from a philosophy course on aesthetics energized and excited. Members in this latter group raved about the quality of the teaching and indicated that they would enjoy taking the course themselves. But as they talked, an uncertainty emerged. After having spent more than an hour in the midst of an intense discussion of the aesthetics of Homer, they were unsure about the current position of philosophers on the question. Yet they were so certain of the quality of this instructor's pedagogical abilities that one of them expressed her confidence that during the next class that the instructor would make clear to the students the consensus philosophers had reached on this subject. At this point FLP fellows from the humanities smiled knowingly and informed their colleagues that nothing of the sort was apt to happen. Instead, the philosophy instructor would most likely begin the following class with a new topic, and once again the class would wander through the possible arguments without ever establishing a particular position as canonical within the discipline. (A later conversation with the philosophy instructor confirmed this interpretation.)

The participants in the FLP seminar immediately recognized that an important chasm existed between those fields in which introductory classes typically revolve around the sharing of an established certainty, recognized by all those in a field, and disciplines in which classes at any level can consist of explorations of various perspectives on an issue without any perceived need to resolve these views into a single insight. If students brought to an introductory science class the kinds of expectations that were appropriate to most humanities courses, they might enjoy the ride through the evidence without ever realizing that there was a single, established explanation that must be understood. By contrast, a student with the perspective of a scientist might wait in vain for the punch line of the accepted interpretation and remain completely oblivious to the process of viewing things from multiple interpretations that was essential for success in the humanities. Either mismatch between the students' expectations and the nature of the discipline could have disastrous consequences for learning, but not one of the seasoned teachers in the FLP seminar had ever explicitly addressed this issue in a course.

Decoding rests on the assumption that there are thousands of such potential mismatches between students' expectations of what they are supposed to do in a course and the actual tasks that are required for success. It is as if our students were to enter the field suited up for a game of field hockey and never quite grasped that they were expected to be playing football. Our experience working in a wide variety of fields suggests that this is not so different from what many students are actually doing in our courses. They never grasp the rules of the discipline, and they never successfully receive cues that indicate that a very different approach to working in this area is required.

This state of affairs immediately raises a second question: Why are students not being presented the "rules of the game" in the discipline? If behind most bottlenecks there is something that has not been taught, why aren't the operating instructions automatically provided at the beginning of each course? This problem does not arise because instructors are ignorant of their fields, nor is it the result of any desire on the part of instructors to prevent students from functioning effectively. Teachers typically enter the classroom able to perform all the steps that students need to function effectively in their fields and willing to share their discipline with their students. And they often make an attempt at the beginning of the semester to tell their students what needs to be done. They note that the class will be reading and analyzing certain texts, but their students have no idea what *reading* and *analyzing* mean in this context. Or they try to suggest what quantitative methods will be used in the course, but the students lack an understanding of how to apply these procedures in the discipline they are supposed to inhabit. The students remain as oblivious to what is actually supposed to happen in the course as were the scientists visiting the philosophy class.

In part this problem arises because instructors tend to concentrate on transmitting the content of their disciplines and to skip over the actual procedures used to create knowledge in the field. As Nancy Chick has written, such pedagogies model "the product rather than the process, as the professor has done the disciplinary work without showing the students how to do the work themselves" (2009, 45). When students in such classes are asked to actually do work in the discipline, their knowledge of the necessary processes is often far too limited for them to succeed.

This emphasis on product rather than process generally derives from a belief that learning problems are primarily about what students do not *know,* whereas our work with decoding rests on the assumption that in most situations it is more useful to focus on what students cannot *do.* In every discipline there are crucial mental operations that must be mastered before the content is meaningful. Until these ways of functioning are grasped, piling on content has little purpose. In history, for example, instructors sometimes complain that students do not know dates. Yet when pressed, few of them are satisfied when students simply memorize a list of years and events. Historians want their students to make use of dates in a particular way that is to a certain extent specific to the discipline. And what students are supposed to actually do with dates turns out to be a much more complex set of mental operations than reciting memorized chronologies. Until students have mastered the series of steps that historians automatically use to relate time to trends and events, they will not be able to succeed in any but the most elementary college history courses.

Ironically, focusing primarily on content may in some cases even keep instructors from incorporating material that the students need to know. Traditionally, subjects were included in a course because they existed on some imagined list of topics that had to be mentioned. When a course is approached from the perspective of what students need to be able to do, by contrast, not only is some content seen to be less important, but other information emerges as essential that may not have been touched upon at all. A systems analyst, for example, asked her students to explore the ways in which a computer program needed to be adapted to the needs of different potential users. But when she decoded this part of her course, it became clear that some of the necessary steps required information about the needs of such users that was not part of the course and was probably not part of the general cultural knowledge of the students. It was clear that, if this work was going to remain a part of the course, new content about the use of such systems had to be added.

Beneath the pedagogical tradition of teaching the product—not the process— is a deeper problem, however. Paradoxically, the very expertise that gives instructors something to teach may in itself make it more difficult to convey the process of actually operating in the discipline. This is a natural result of the manner in which the human brain masters complex tasks. In order to operate at a higher level, many lower-level mental processes must occur automatically. When driving a car, the physical act of turning the steering wheel or judging the distance between vehicles normally occurs without conscious thought, while attention is focused on other challenges, such as evaluating the behavior of other drivers or confirming the speed limit. For those just learning to drive, however, such basic operations need to be foregrounded and performed consciously and carefully.

This process, which is entirely functional in itself, can become a problem when the expert enters the classroom. Functioning as physicists or literary critics has become so natural and automatic to instructors that many of the most essential operations needed to function in the field have become invisible to them. In the example of the FLP fellows mentioned earlier, it is unlikely to occur to scientists that their students might not be looking for the state-of-the-art explanation of a phenomenon, or to humanists that their students are ignoring the process of viewing a question from different perspectives because they are waiting to hear which view is correct. Therefore, these essential steps are never taught, and the resulting failures are attributed to lack of effort or ability.

The invisibility of crucial steps is exacerbated by the fact that most instructors have found their subjects easier to master in the first place than do many of their students. For these instructors, basic elements in the discipline may have been assimilated so quickly and so painlessly that they left little mark on consciousness. Moreover, as Leah Shopkow has pointed out, the nature of professional training itself contributes to the disappearance from consciousness of crucial mental operations. Training in PhD programs is typically conducted in small seminars in which future college instructors have an opportunity to absorb the practices of the discipline through direct contact with an expert in the field, and in this kind of face-to-face apprenticeship many of the steps required for such work may never have been explicitly set forth (Shopkow et al. 2013a).

Ironically, it is because many elements of disciplinary expertise have become so "natural" to the teacher that they are not immediately available for conscious scrutiny. Like the purloined letter in Edgar Allan Poe's famous story, they are not seen *because* they are so obvious. This natural tendency to remove basic processes from consciousness leads instructors to leave crucial steps untaught. They tend to share those elements of a discipline that they themselves consciously employ when doing research while skipping over those that are so automatic that they remain unconscious. To use a biological analogy, it is as if instructors are trying to pass on the intellectual inheritance of the field, but there are gaps in the genomic sequence they are transmitting.

The subjective experience of students in this situation is well expressed in an insightful observation from a mathematics student in the United Kingdom:

> Once they start heading off into realms of genius, you get people who have been locked in their room studying one equation for fifteen years but cannot contemplate where you are on this learning curve and don't understand what they're teaching you is utterly foreign, utterly random, and they can't understand how you can't understand it. (Quoted in Land et al. 2006, 199–200)

However, this passage does not capture the full nature of the problem. At least the student who produced this comment was aware of the fact that he or she did not fully grasp what was expected. The situation is even worse for those students who are unaware that their understanding of what is required for success in the discipline is fundamentally flawed. Lacking a complete model for operating in the discipline, they make incorrect assumptions about what is called for in a course and, as a result, do quite badly.

The notion that the tacit nature of expert knowledge may create problems for students is not unique to decoding. John Bransford and his colleagues, for example, have argued that "expertise can sometimes hurt teaching because many experts forget what is easy and what is difficult for students" (Bransford, Brown, and Cocking 2000, 44). But while this problem has been recognized, it has rarely been made the core of a systematic effort to identify and to respond to those places where an instructor's expertise gets in the way of the students' learning. For Decoding the Disciplines, this project is central.

So long as an instructor is not fully aware of the crucial steps in the disciplinary process that are being omitted from teaching, it is difficult to remedy the situation. Thus, it is essential for those seeking to overcome bottlenecks to student learning to become conscious of what remains untaught in their classes. Encounters with patterns of instruction in very different disciplines, such as that in the story of the FLP fellows described earlier in this chapter, can be surprisingly helpful in sensitizing instructors to the need to make explicit hidden ways of operating in their own discipline, and readers of this book are strongly encouraged to experiment with visiting classes in other fields.

Unfortunately, such experiences are rarely sufficient in themselves. If we are to really help students, we need to have a clearer notion of the mental operations that they must master to get past specific bottlenecks in particular courses. Understanding these can revolutionize our teaching, but many of these operations are so deeply buried in the unconscious of our disciplines that serious and systematic intellectual labor is needed to make us aware of the steps that we need to teach our students. It was to address this problem that the decoding interview was developed. But the interview process is a complex undertaking, and it is necessary to analyze it in some detail. (Further examples of decoding interviews may be seen at http://decodingthedisciplines.org/step-2-uncover-the-mental-task/).

The Decoding Interview 1: Making Operations Explicit

At the very core of the decoding endeavor is the notion that a special process is necessary to make conscious many of the basic operations that must be taught to students. Several techniques have been developed to achieve this goal, but the most thorough is the decoding interview. The form of this investigation into the disciplinary unconscious is deceptively simple. An instructor is asked to clearly describe a place in a course where many students get stuck, and the interviewer asks the question, "What would *you* do if you were asked to complete the task that blocks your students' learning?" The initial responses are generally relatively superficial, so the interviewer presses the instructor to go a deeper level, asking, "*How* do you do that?" The interviewer continues in this vein, with the instructor describing increasingly basic mental operations and the interviewers pressing for complex steps to be broken up into their component parts.

Before beginning to explore in detail the techniques needed in this process, let us view a very effective description of her own interview by Sally Haney, who teaches journalism at Mount Royal University:

> I agreed to participate in a research project in which I was decoded by two non-journalist colleagues. That interview was a game-changer. To help illustrate how the method surfaced some of my own ingrained knowledge, I share below a snapshot of my experience, aided by a snippet of the interview transcript. As I prepared for my decoding interview, I was asked to think carefully

about a bottleneck to student learning in my classes. My response came quickly—story ideas. For years, I have witnessed students struggle to consistently generate strong journalistic pitches. We show them good work. We provide questions they should address in their pitches. We engage in many conversations with them about audience, story tension, and public interest. We discuss focus, angles, and hooks. Sometimes, in return, we hear them articulate strong ideas. Other times, the ideas are weak. They lack tension, are poorly researched, are much too big or much too small. When the decoders pushed me to define the bottleneck more clearly, I eventually concluded that it related to pattern recognition—that students struggle to recognize the patterns that are often consistent with strong story ideas. The decoders also asked me many questions about what I did as an "expert" to generate my own story ideas. I was repeatedly asked to describe in detail how I went about the process. This hour-long conversation resulted in some key takeaways, including the degree to which my ideas were usually connected to breaks in established patterns. In other words, issues, events, and people typically appeared on my story radar when they struck me as different from the norm. The decoding experience allowed me to see how quickly and often I had taken away the opportunity for students to identify and practise finding these breaks in patterns. (Haney 2015)

The goal of the interview is always to make explicit the hidden mental operations that are necessary to successfully complete the work in a course and to break these skills down into their component parts. But this process is considerably more demanding than might at first appear. In practice, the central question "How do you do that?" morphs into many different forms to match the context.

EXAMPLES OF QUESTIONS FROM DECODING INTERVIEWS

Here are a few of the variations of the question "How do you do that?" that might be appropriate as particular interviews unfold:

What does that tell you?
What information are you getting from that?
How do you know which element of the problem to focus on first?
What are you looking for at this point?
Are you visualizing anything as you do that?
Why is doing that important?
How does the response to this action affect what you do next?
How do you know what to ignore at this point?
Are you comparing what you see here to something else?
How do you know which method to apply at this point?
How do you know when you have hit a dead end?

Interviewers must be careful to avoid being mesmerized by digressions into the content of the field or leaps to a consideration of how particular steps might be taught, as compelling as these may be. Instead, the interviewee must be led gently, but firmly, back to the definition of crucial metal operations. It is generally best to use two interviewers because it is easy to get lost in the details, and because two minds can keep the process on track better than one. We have also found that it is best if at least one of them comes from a field outside the discipline of the interviewee. There is always a danger that members of the same field will share common blind spots, and an interviewer from outside the discipline is better able to see what has not been fully explained.

Interviewers must pay constant attention to the nature of the responses to be sure that crucial steps are not being left out and that disciplinary jargon is replaced with simple descriptions of the steps that must be taken to complete the task at hand. Experts in every field tend to operate like engineers or computer scientists, inserting "black boxes" in diagrams to represent subprocesses that are not explained in detail. This process is entirely functional for those who are already well versed in the field, but it can be baffling to the novice. Therefore, interviewers must watch very carefully for places in which the steps are being skipped over, because these are often the very mental operations that are apt to be missing in students' understanding of the discipline. When such absences appear in the account of the instructor, interviewers must be ready to return to the central question, "But *how* do you do that?"

An Example of a Decoding Interview

It is easy to get the impression that the decoding interview is a simple linear process, whereas in practice the interviewee often wanders away from the central task and needs to be drawn back to making explicit the mental operations required for success in the course. This is natural, since the instructor being interviewed is not generally accustomed to approaching the issue in this particular fashion. But it is necessary for the interviewers to keep drawing the conversation back to the task of revealing the steps that students must master to succeed in the course.

To provide a sense of the meandering nature of most interviews, I have included a segment from an interview below and an analysis of the moves that were being made to reveal the hidden mental operations that needed to be taught to students. In these excerpts from one of the interviews conducted by the Indiana University History Learning Project (HLP), a historian focused on the difficulty that his students had in using an oral epic to understand traditional societies in a region in Africa—a task that might be challenging even to professional historians in other fields. But, given the nature of available sources, this kind of analysis is a necessary part of understanding the history of these peoples.

In reading this transcript, note how the interviewers bring the instructor back to the issue of what students must do to operate successfully in a history course. All bracketed comments in italics represent my later commentary on the process.

[*The interviewee has just described a traditional oral epic that he would like his students to use in understanding a society that is being studied.*]

INTERVIEWER 1: That is a great example. Really good. So what do you do when you look at the epic?

[*The instructor initially describes the content of the epic and how he goes about teaching it. He needs to be brought back to the task of explaining what he does with the text.*]

INTERVIEWER 1: Okay. So the next question is to put yourself in the perspective of someone who is in the course who has had all this background material, who sits down to read the text. And what does he or she do? Someone who does it correctly, that is, and someone who is a trained historian.

INSTRUCTOR: Okay. So, the ideal student?

[*The instructor has transferred the focus from the trained professional to the student who has thoroughly mastered disciplinary practices, but, since the process is presumably the same in this case, the interview was continued without interruption.*]

INTERVIEWER 1: What would he or she do? Yes. Right.

INSTRUCTOR: The ideal student would be interested in the story but ask questions about why this very elaborate story happened and why, for example, it is a very conventional story about hunters. [*More details about the story.*] Why is this story very different? [*More details about the story.*] What is being said in this story to have that little detail in it. And so I would hope that the story itself would raise some questions and they start asking about it. What is being said or communicated about genealogy? Are there questions about gender roles clearly in all of this? I would ask questions about who are these people, what other roles they may have played in the epic. So there is more information that I would want, but I would focus in on sort of the peculiarities or the uniqueness of the story and what that might communicate.

INTERVIEWER 1: Okay. So you would put it up against other stories?

INSTRUCTOR: Uh-huh.

As in most interviews, this interaction did not proceed automatically toward its goal. At several points the instructor shifted attention from the mental operations needed to make use of this epic as a historical source to the content of the epic itself. This was a perfectly understandable move for an expert fascinated with this material, and these digressions represented a temptation for the interviewers, who found the material interesting. But they had to discipline themselves to gently draw the instructor back to the process of making explicit the steps that must be mastered to process this oral poem historically.

Within the responses of the interviewee is a description of some of the concrete steps that an African historian would take to process this work. Thus, after the interview we know that, in order to make use of this source, students in this course must:

- Constantly pose questions about the historical significance of the details in this work.
- Have at their disposal a set of questions that they are prepared to pose when elements in the text suggest that they are appropriate. These include:
  - What is the significance of particular details?
  - What is being said or communicated about genealogy?
  - What are the implicit gender roles in the story?
  - Who are the people being described?
  - What other roles did the characters play in the epic?
- Consider how the elements in this epic are like and unlike other parallel stories.

When laid out explicitly, the process of posing questions may seem so obvious to an expert in the field that it is not worth mentioning. But in fact, there is a great deal of evidence that many students bring to college a very different notion of what they are expected to do in history courses (see, for example, Levstik and Barton 2002; Wineburg 2001). Viewing history as a process of collecting and memorizing facts and dates, such students do not understand that posing questions and comparing sources are a crucial part of the process. And even if a realization of the importance of asking questions were to occur to them, they would lack an understanding of what kinds of questions to pose. History instructors generally take such processes for granted and plunge into the content of the course. But an interview of this sort can serve to alert them to the necessity of actually showing students these steps of historical analysis.

If students do not master these general procedures for posing questions, they will be very unlikely to successfully make use of the content. But making these processes explicit would not be the end of this part of the interview process. Each of these mental operations is, in fact, not a simple action but a collection of more specific acts that must be defined more clearly before students can fully actualize these steps. Therefore, it would probably be necessary to present the interviewee with a series of follow-up questions in order to probe more deeply into each of these mental operations:

- At particular points in the text, what suggests to you that a question needs to be posed?
- What tells you which elements in the epic to single out in the search for the story's historical significance?
- How do you go about moving from elements in the story to an understanding of patterns of gender relations in this society?
- How do you go about understanding genealogical relations in the story?
- What do you do with the answers that you get to these questions?
- At a particular point in the reading, what suggests to you that a comparison to a different text or other cultural artifact might be useful in your analysis of this particular source?
- How do you know which other text or artifact to pick for comparison?
- When you are comparing the original text with something else, what are you looking for?
- When you have detected a set of similarities and/or differences, what is the next step?

Theoretically, this questioning process could continue indefinitely, like the four-year-old who asks "Why?" to every explanation that is offered. But at some point, one arrives at a level that the participants agree is so basic that it seems likely the operations would be understandable to any student who has the cognitive skills expected at that level in the educational system. If, however, later assessments of student performance indicate that attempts to model these operations are not successful, it may be necessary to return to the decoding process and break up these operations into steps that are even easier to manage.

The details of this interview are, of course, specific to history and, to a certain extent, to the subfield of African history. But the general process of breaking complex and ill-defined tasks into a series of clearly defined mental operations is applicable to any discipline. As we shall see in subsequent chapters, once this has been done, it is much easier to present students with the steps that they must employ, to provide them with opportunities to practice these mental operations, and to assess the learners' mastery of each. And this process of making explicit and breaking down the required tasks can increase student effort in the course, since students facing clearly defined and manageable challenges are more likely to be motivated than those who are trying to function in the midst of vague and seemingly impossible demands.

The Decoding Interview 2: Strategies for Digging Deeper

In the process of conducting well over a hundred decoding interviews, we have found that certain strategies are effective in bringing an interview to a successful conclusion. It is, for example, very important to remain alert for places where the instructor is continuing to use abstractions that mask the actual mental operations that students must master. Some interviewers have done this by imagining themselves performing the task that is the occasion for the bottleneck; if they are unable to see how they themselves would go about this work, then they know that the instructor has not presented all the necessary steps. Others remain on the lookout for large, vague, and complex descriptions of the task at hand and then work with the instructor to break these up into their component parts. If, for example, a scientist complains that students have difficulty seeing the implications of data presented in a graph, an interviewer operating in this fashion will note the vague and undefined terms *seeing* and *implications* and press the instructor to be more specific about what it means to *see* in this context and how one goes about moving from the lines on a graph to the *implications* that a professional in the field would automatically draw from them. The appearance of disciplinary jargon that would not be completely clear to someone outside the field is also often a good indication that it is time to ask the instructor to explain more explicitly what students must do to get past the bottleneck.

Certain kinds of questions have also proven to be particularly useful in making operations explicit in a wide range of disciplines:

- In a particular situation being described, how does one distinguish between essential elements and details?
- Are there particular kinds of questions that experts in the discipline automatically bring to a problem?
- How do those in the field move back and forth between verbal and mathematical descriptions of a problem?
- How do practitioners deal with issues of ambiguity?
- How does one test the validity of a thesis/hypothesis in this area of knowledge or establish connections between different elements?

Such questions can often create real turning points in interviews and reveal necessary steps that had previously remained unconscious.

A particularly useful type of question involves the use of visualization in decoding—an area that Joan Middendorf has pioneered. In many academic fields, experts "see" phenomena in ways that may be so automatic to them that they never recognize that it is necessary to make this step explicit to students. Sometimes these visualizations are static, and sometimes they are animated. Molecular biologists often imagine proteins moving and interacting in a cell. Geologists transform the strata they observe into moving pictures of continents colliding and water eroding on a scale of millions of years. If students are not introduced to these ways of processing information, they misunderstand entirely what they need to do to succeed in a course.

It is also important to pay attention to the general structure of the exchange. Often near the beginning of an interview, the instructor will make a statement that contains several "black boxes." In such cases it is necessary to focus on one of these and reduce it to more basic mental operations before returning to the other operations that need decoding. For example, early in an interview an instructor teaching a course on taxation might say that, unlike many students, experts in the field know that there may be more than one valid answer to a tax question and that issues outside tax law may need to be considered (e.g., financial issues, tax risk tolerance, or ethics). The interviewers might seize on the first statement and probe to see just how professionals in the field go about recognizing different potential interpretations of a situation. This part of the interview could easily take thirty minutes or more if blocks are encountered along the way and the instructor has to work hard to make his or her mental practices explicit. But it would be very important for the interviewers to keep in mind the other issue (how tax accountants decide what issues outside tax law itself might be relevant to a particular case) and to systematically explore it after the first issue has been reduced to its elements (Middendorf, Shopkow, Pace, Barnett, and Timmermans 2014).

The Decoding Interview 3: Personal Interactions

Early in the development of decoding we began using the term *interview* to describe the process through which the implicit mental operations within disciplinary practices were made explicit, and in many ways this exchange does resemble the kinds of intellectual dialogues that we encounter in other aspects of contemporary culture. But unlike most interviews, which aim to make explicit ideas and impressions that the interviewee already possesses at the beginning of the process, the goal of this interaction is to bring the subject to a new understanding of his or her professional work. In this sense the form of the interview, although obviously not its content, often resembles that of certain types of psychotherapy.

Decoding interviews are unlike traditional psychoanalysis in that the knowledge that is being brought to the surface has not been actively repressed, and there is no part of the self that is invested in keeping this knowledge secret. Nonetheless, there can be an active resistance to the procedure. The intellectual process of making conscious the hidden mental operations required for success in a discipline can be quite exhilarating, but it is also tiring and, sometimes, even threatening to the interviewee. Academics depend on their grasp of their disciplines, and it can be difficult for them to come face to face with the fact that there are some aspects of their fields that they cannot immediately explain.

The emotional experience of the interviewee has effectively been captured by journalism educator Sally Haney (2015), who notes, "Decoding (and being decoded)

THE FLOW OF AN INTERVIEW

Here is a schematic diagram of a hypothetical interview with an accountant about the steps that students need to master to overcome a bottleneck in responding to issues in tax law. (In practice, each step might consist of multiple questions and answers.)

  At a certain point two different "black boxes" appear. The first is unpacked, and then the interviewer moves on to the second. The arrows indicate the order in which the interview might unfold.*

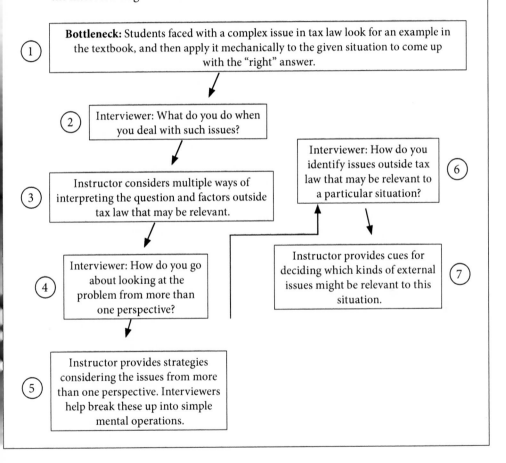

1. **Bottleneck:** Students faced with a complex issue in tax law look for an example in the textbook, and then apply it mechanically to the given situation to come up with the "right" answer.

2. Interviewer: What do you do when you deal with such issues?

3. Instructor considers multiple ways of interpreting the question and factors outside tax law that may be relevant.

4. Interviewer: How do you go about looking at the problem from more than one perspective?

5. Instructor provides strategies considering the issues from more than one perspective. Interviewers help break these up into simple mental operations.

6. Interviewer: How do you identify issues outside tax law that may be relevant to a particular situation?

7. Instructor provides cues for deciding which kinds of external issues might be relevant to this situation.

---

* Special thanks to James Barnett and Julie Timmermans (2014) for the material from which this example was drawn.

is time-consuming and difficult work. When my interview concluded, I was exhausted. I was also excited about examining my expertise to better assist my students in their learning. At the same time, I felt vulnerable, even embarrassed, because after years of teaching, there I was, struggling to explain a core concept."

It is thus very important to establish a relationship of trust with the person being interviewed. Interviewers must combine their efforts to press instructors for the clearest possible statement of the necessary operations with frequent reassurance that the process is going well. The interviewee should be reminded both at the beginning and at various points in the interview that an initial inability to answer a question is a positive indication that the process is succeeding in entering the disciplinary unconscious. Images of exploring new territory or creating new technologies of learning can be useful in creating an emotional climate in which not being able to provide instant answers is less threatening.

It can also be disturbing for dedicated instructors to realize that they have been teaching a subject for years without providing students with some of the necessary tools for mastering the material. This can often generate feelings of guilt or a desire to jump prematurely to the search for new ways to teach newly uncovered steps to students, but either of these responses can derail the process. Thus, it is often important to reassure instructors that they have not been alone in overlooking steps that needed to be taught and that they are contributing to our collective understanding of how to reach students by participating in the interview.

The emotional and intellectual complexity of the interactions also requires interviewers to become quite agile. They must always be on the lookout for op-

---

CONDUCTING A DECODING INTERVIEW:
SUGGESTIONS FOR INTERVIEWERS

1. Ask the interviewee-expert to describe a bottleneck to learning in one of his or her courses.
2. Ask the expert to explain how he or she would go about performing the task that is difficult for many students.
3. Imagine yourself doing what is being described, or ask yourself if crucial steps are being left out.
4. Summarize what the expert says; restate it.
5. Ask questions when you don't understand; probe when the expert cannot explain something or when crucial steps seem to have been left out.
6. Reassure the expert.
7. Gently interrupt if the expert talks about how to teach this material to students or starts to lecture on content.

portunities to unearth more hidden mental operations, but also aware when it is time to back off temporarily if the interviewee seems to be feeling threatened. Interviewers must be watching for connections between elements that have already emerged at the same time that they are alert to what is not being included. They must be aware of when it is time to test a particular hunch with the interviewee to see if it will lead to a greater understanding of the hidden processes of the discipline or when it is best to remain silent and see where the subject will go on his or her own. And they must accept the fact that some interviewees will simply not ever make the commitment to exploring their own ignorance—a commitment that is necessary for the process to be effective.

All of this makes the decoding interview a demanding task that requires great concentration; indeed, veteran decoders often report that there is a limit to the number of interviews that they can perform in a week. But the interview can also be a source of emotional and intellectual satisfaction. When all is going well, it can be one of the most enjoyable aspects of the decoding process.

Finally, it should be noted that the decoding interview also has a secondary value. Beyond simply unearthing the implicit mental operations students need, it can deepen an instructor's involvement with teaching. The search for these hidden elements often transforms student learning into a fascinating intellectual puzzle and can evoke the elements of curiosity and challenge that make traditional disciplinary research so compelling for those in academia. Thus, instructors often emerge from the interviews with both a new excitement about teaching and a transformed sense of the unity of these two aspects of academic life.

Beyond the Interview

The "classic" decoding interview described above continues to be one of the most effective tools for making explicit the basic operations necessary for success in a discipline. But it is time consuming and requires skill on the part of the interviewer and commitment on that of the instructor. If every improvement in every course required the full process, the interview itself could, ironically, become a bottleneck in the process of increasing learning about learning.

Fortunately there are ways around this problem. First, as we shall see in more depth in chapter 7, the power of community can be used to facilitate the process of making explicit the disciplinary unconscious. As the work of the HLP indicates, it is possible for a few members of a discipline to conduct extensive research, involving multiple interviews, and then to share this with others in the field through presentations, publications, and websites. It will still be necessary for individual instructors to evaluate whether the mental operations that have been unearthed are relevant to the particular courses that they are teaching. But much of the heavy lifting will have already been accomplished.

Second, considerable work has already been devoted to creating alternative paths to hidden mental operations, when the full interview process is impractical. A very creative response to this problem has been created by Swantje Lahm and Svenja Kaduk at the University of Bielefeld (2016). Building on work by Sondra Perl (2004), Lahm and Kaduk translated the interview process into a writing exercise in which individuals respond to prompts about the mental operations in their disciplines and then periodically discuss what they are learning with other members of a group. This has the advantage of working with a number of instructors simultaneously, and it also provides a safe space in which individuals can explore these learning issues without having to make public more than they feel comfortable sharing. This approach is particularly useful in situations in which the institutional or cultural context, or the political realities of a unit discourage teachers from openly sharing difficulties they are having in the classroom.

In chapter 7 we will see more examples of ways in which the mental operations in a discipline can be systematically explored in a group setting, but it is worth noting here that in her work with faculty at the Indiana University Center for Innovation in Teaching, Joan Middendorf has developed two techniques—decoding through rubrics and through metaphors—that provide useful alternatives to the full decoding interview. Both of these will be treated briefly below and will be presented more thoroughly in Joan Middendorf and Leah Shopkow's forthcoming volume *Decoding the Disciplines: How to Help Students Learn Critical Thinking.*

Decoding through Rubrics

An important alternative to the decoding interview is the use of rubrics to make visible the kinds of mental operations that are required for success in a particular course. The instructor begins by listing mistakes that students have actually made in attempting to complete a particular task. Then, opposite each type of mistake, the instructor writes what must be done to avoid the error. This second list provides the starting point for defining the mental operations that are essential in the course. In this approach an essential role is played by someone outside the discipline who engages with the instructor in a discussion of the student errors and the corresponding operations that must be mastered. The resulting rubric of positive operations can serve as a road map for the course, directing the instructor toward the essential skills that need to be modeled.

To give one example, students kept daily journals for an overseas study course that compared U.S. and French design aesthetics. The rubric of student mistakes produced by the instructor included listing what was seen without explanation, limiting analysis to discussion points from class tours, and photographic "selfies." Each of these absences of a student skill could provide the occasion for an analysis of precisely what disciplinary operations had not been mastered.

This approach has two advantages that makes it particularly useful to educational developers. First, it requires less initial commitment than the formal interview. A rubric exercise does not require an explanation of the entire decoding apparatus, though it can easily be followed by a fuller discussion of the approach. Second, it can be accomplished in a short period of time and with groups of faculty who can help make each other's operations clear. It is, however, generally necessary for someone besides the instructor—preferably someone from outside the discipline—to work with this material, assuring that hidden mental operations are made explicit and that large tasks are broken down into their constituent parts.

Decoding through Metaphors

As we shall see in chapter 3, metaphors can play an important role in the modeling of basic operations. But, as Joan Middendorf has effectively demonstrated, the creation of metaphors can also provide an alternative mechanism for making explicit some of the mental operations in the field that might otherwise not be conveyed to students. Instructors who have not decoded their disciplines are often speaking a language their students do not understand. When these instructors are asked to provide a metaphor for the operations that confuse students, they must leave the linguistic echo chamber of their field and describe these ways of functioning in a broader language that can be more easily be understood.

When experts in history, for example, attempt to describe the difficulties some of their students have in organizing information about a particular period, they might say that students lump everything together, have no understanding of either change or continuity, and view everything from the perspective of their own time. Such comments may in a certain sense be accurate, but they are vague and do not provide a basis for a serious effort to model these operations for students. When historians are pressed to provide a metaphor for such mental operations, however, they might suggest that these processes are like the work on an archaeological dig. If they are encouraged to explain more precisely what the two domains share, they might reply that just as the archaeologist carefully notes the strata at which particular artifacts are found, the historian constantly brings together sources from the same time period. Both activities involve the reconstruction of connections between different elements from the same period and attention to continuity and change across periods, and both are sensitive to ways in which different groups or regions in the same period did or did not share similar ways of life. Each of the elements revealed through this comparison can then be individually modeled for students (step 3), and opportunities to practice each can be provided (step 4). And, as an extra bonus, the metaphor of the archaeological dig could be used in class to make clearer to students what is being expected of them (step 3).

Thus, the systematic development of metaphors with experts in a field can begin a process of uncovering the mental operations in a discipline. The particular metaphors that emerge will be dictated by the nature of the field and that of the material being taught, but each can serve to help instructors or scholars of teaching and learning to delve deeper into the nature of that discipline and to arrive at specific ways of operating that are necessary for success in the field. Like rubrics, metaphors can serve to draw instructors into the decoding process with minimal initial explanation or commitment. They are relatively simple, and may provide the "aha!" insights that will encourage further exploration of the bottlenecks and mental operations of a field.

Using Existing Scholarship of Teaching and Learning to Identify Mental Operations

As we have seen, the decoding process can add precision to the effort to identify those mental operations that are essential in a particular course. Yet, for some time, scholars of teaching and learning have been seeking to analyze disciplinary learning within other contexts of discovery. These efforts to specify the ways of thinking in particular disciplines can provide a very valuable asset to anyone involved in decoding. In many cases it will be necessary to sharpen these definitions and to translate descriptions of general skills into specific mental actions that students must master. But building on studies done within other frameworks of analysis can often greatly speed up the process of decoding and generate valuable insights independently of the paradigm.

A case in point is Sherry Linkon's excellent study *Literary Learning* (2011). In her analysis of the elements of literary thinking, Linkon defines a number of the essential orientations that scholars automatically bring to the process of studying literature. She argues that they view literature as "an opportunity to see the world through someone's eyes and, in the process, understand ourselves better" (9). Literary scholars focus on context, they recognize that literature is complex, and they view literature as a construction and remain aware of the presence of the author. They embrace complexity, ambiguity, and subjectivity, and they welcome a variety of approaches to understanding texts. Experts in this area are self-conscious about the way they approach their sources and consider alternative strategies for finding meaning. Linkon devotes pages to the analysis of the reading practices and patterns of argumentation used by experts in the field, even considering the specialized vocabulary that must be mastered to function effectively within it.

Each point in Linkon's careful dissection of literary practice could be the focus for a decoding analysis. In such an analysis it would be necessary to map these basic mental operations onto the patterns of bottlenecks in a specific course to be sure that one is addressing those elements that are creating problems for the particular group of students in one's own course. In some cases it would be necessary to probe deeper to determine precisely what experts in the field actually do when they see the world through the eyes of another, embrace ambiguity, and so on. And it may be necessary to break some of these large mental operations into their constituent parts. But it is clear that Linkon has already done a great deal of the hard mental work required to define what students have do to succeed in a course in this area. Anyone attempting to decode a course in literary studies could avoid much of the initial effort required in this endeavor by beginning with her analysis and then moving forward within the decoding framework.

Sometimes the use of existing scholarship on teaching and learning for identifying key disciplinary operations is more indirect. Gerald Graff and Cathy Birkenstein are justly celebrated for the creation of concrete exercises that provide undergraduates with opportunities to practice some of the fundamental rhetorical moves of expository writing. But the practical exercises in their *They Say/I Say* (2006) implicitly rest on a very careful theoretical analysis of the steps that experts take to produce effective prose. Through a kind of reverse engineering it is possible to work backward from their specific exercises to the mental operations that underlie these moves. For example, in suggesting the kinds of verbs that students could use in different situations—making a claim, expressing agreement, questioning or disagreeing, and making recommendations—Graff and Birkenstein are implicitly giving us access to several essential steps performed automatically by expert writers. As was observed in the discussion of Linkon's work, each of these points could become the subject of a decoding exercise. How, for example, do scholars in the field make a claim? What forms of agreement, questioning, or disagreement are acceptable in the discipline? Such an inquiry could make explicit crucial steps that are so elementary that they are invisible to expert writers, and, thus, remain untaught (Graff and Birkenstein 2006, 39–40).

Thus, the rapidly growing work within the scholarship of teaching and learning is providing an invaluable resource for anyone seeking to define the mental operations that students much master to succeed in particular fields. Reconsidering such scholarship from the perspective of decoding can provide a powerful tool for increasing student learning.

Decoding and the Epistemology of a Discipline

Even building on the work of other scholars of teaching and learning, decoding could seem an endless and frustrating process if every single operation in a discipline had to be laboriously brought to consciousness and then carefully modeled, practiced, and assessed. Step 1 of the process would, of course, greatly narrow the work, since the focus on bottlenecks would eliminate from consideration many aspects of the field that were not proving to be problematic for students. Even so, a typical investigation of a single bottleneck can unearth a number of different operations, each of which would need to be taught, and a course can have multiple bottlenecks.

The work of the History Learning Project (HLP) strongly suggests, however, that in practice the task is much less daunting because the problems faced in conveying the essence of a discipline are linked to one another, and solving one can have a beneficial effect on others. As we probed deeper into the discipline, my HLP colleague Leah Shopkow came to the realization that the great majority of problems that keep students from mastering a field result from a misunderstanding of its epistemology (Shopkow 2010; Shopkow et al. 2013a, 2013b). When students do not understand the specific mechanisms of thought that produce historical knowledge, they make a great number of mistakes. In the case of history, many students operate as if understanding the past was a matter of piling hard, incontrovertible facts on top of each other until the truth of history is obvious to any rational human being. When asked to perform many tasks that are natural to historians, such as dealing with ambiguous evidence or comparing the relative merits of two historical interpretations, they make many different kinds of errors. But all of these mistakes go back to the central misunderstanding about what is entailed in the creation of knowledge in the discipline.

If Shopkow's crucial insight holds for other disciplines (and we have considerable evidence that it does), the task of decoding becomes much easier. When instructors isolate a crucial mental operation and assist students in mastering it, they are quite often also teaching students something fundamental about the epistemology of the discipline. In helping students master the use of evidence in a history course, for example, an instructor is simultaneously teaching them something about the manner in which historians generate interpretations, defend or criticize arguments, and organize their writing, because all of these practices are based in a common epistemological orientation. This revised understanding of the discipline can lead students to avoid other bottlenecks on their own. Thus, by dealing in depth with a few central learning problems in a course, other potential difficulties may disappear spontaneously.

Like the exploration of rubrics and metaphors, the understanding of the role of epistemology in the generation of bottlenecks is a work in progress, and hopefully in the near future we will see more from Shopkow about this highly important topic.

Making the Shift to Exploring Operations

To make full use of the decoding paradigm, a major conceptual shift is needed. Instructors must begin to see bottlenecks as windows into the workings of their students' minds (step 1), and they must conceptualize the sharing of their disciplines as a matter not only of simply conveying knowledge but also of instilling certain patterns of mind in their students—patterns that are generally quite specific to their discipline. And, perhaps most important, they must see teaching as an intellectually demanding undertaking that requires the same kinds of deep analysis that are necessary for traditional disciplinary research.

Once mastered, however, decoding can allow teachers to present discipline-specific thinking in a clear and effective way. Instructors who have made this paradigm shift may wonder how they could have ever taught without first systematically exploring the underlying mental processes they want students to learn. With practice, the examination of the mental operations of experts can become the basic foundation for planning instruction and curricula.

But the question remains: how precisely can we restructure students' conception of our fields? If the first two stages of decoding have been conducted successfully, we have identified a place where the learning of many students is blocked, and we have broken that large, global task into a series of well-defined mental operations. The next step is to identify the most effective strategies for modeling these ways of operating for our students, and that will be the topic of chapter 3.

3. MODELING OPERATIONS

IN THE FIRST step of Decoding the Disciplines we identified those problem areas where learning is not occurring. In the second step we explored the mental operations that students need to master to get past these bottlenecks. These steps focus attention on the places where the decoding process is most needed and define what must be taught. They replace the single-minded emphasis on conveying content, which is so natural for many instructors, with a stress on those mental operations that are necessary for understanding and processing that content.

But, as essential as these steps are, in isolation they remain mere intellectual exercises. Recognizing the particular skills needed in a course does nothing in itself; it only affects learning when these essential disciplinary operations are successfully transmitted to students. We must therefore find effective ways to model these ways of operating for students, and this brings us squarely back into the realm of teaching.

Preparation for Modeling

Before we can plunge into the process of sharing with students the mental operations required for success in a course, we must organize and prioritize the insights that were gained in steps 1 and 2. First, it is necessary to put content temporarily out of one's mind. Later, after decisions have been made concerning which mental operations to model, appropriate content can readily be found to use as examples, and opportunities can be found to provide students with the necessary background. But at this point in the process it is important to remain concentrated on what students must be taught to do, not what they must know.

As was noted in chapters 1 and 2, the first step of the decoding process usually produces a large number of specific operations that students need to master—too many to be explicitly taught in a single course. Therefore, it is important to decide which of these are most likely to stand in the way of further learning and to concentrate on them. If these ways of functioning in the discipline are effectively taught, students will frequently be able to overcome lesser bottlenecks on their own with only limited input from the instructor. The determination of which operations are most essential is always provisional. If at the end of the decoding

---

PREPARATION FOR MODELING

- Temporarily put the content of the course out of mind.
- Pick the most essential operations to model.
- Generally avoid modeling more than one operation at a time.
- Be prepared to later model the integration of already established operations into more complex procedures.

---

process it is clear that major bottlenecks to learning remain, it may be necessary to reassess whether some of the mental processes that were ignored in the initial effort were in fact more essential than had been assumed.

Once the mental operations to be conveyed have been selected, it is important to be sure that one is dealing with basic operations on a sufficiently detailed level. As has been noted repeatedly in previous chapters, one of the real advantages of the first two steps in the decoding process is that large, complex tasks are broken into components that are much easier for students to master. But this only works if specificity is maintained in the process of modeling. Thus, one typically shows students how to do one simple mental operation at a time, or at most a couple of related operations. Rather than attempting to model at one stroke all aspects of writing a paper, for example, this complex task must be first broken down into its constituent parts—considering what must be demonstrated to make a thesis credible or identifying evidence that would aid that process. Once this series of micro-operations has been carefully taught to students, they can be shown how to integrate these processes in a more complex task.

The Modeling Process

Modeling can be one of the most enjoyable and creative parts of the decoding process. It often allows instructors to more effectively share what they find most exciting about working in their fields, and it can open the way for students to do the kinds of serious thinking in the discipline that teachers love to see. The fact that the goal of the teaching has been clearly defined and reduced to manageable units via the first two steps makes the process much easier and efficient. But it is still important to pay close attention to the manner in which the targeted operations are presented to students.

As we shall see in the next section of this chapter, modeling should be pervasive and shape every part of a course from the syllabus to the final exam. But it is also important to sometimes devote a section of a class entirely to the presentation of a particular mental operation or limited set of related operations. This typically involves three elements: (1) instructors provide a metaphor or analogy that helps make clearer the kind of thinking that is being taught;[1] (2) they perform the operations in front of the students; and (3) they make metacomments throughout that label each part of the process so that students understand that they are being presented with steps that they themselves should reproduce.

A particularly effective use of a metaphor to model basic operations was employed in a course on creative writing by Tony Ardizzone, now an emeritus professor in the Indiana University–Bloomington Department of English. He began a class on writing poetry by describing a short story by Abioseh Nicol in which a couple in a traditional African society decide to get married. Following custom, the bride-to-be returns to the house of her family, and the future husband comes asking for her. The family brings out a cousin, a sister, and a succession of female relatives, but the suitor refuses each one until the right one appears.

This process, Ardizzone told his class, resembles in many ways that of writing a poem as the poet considers a series of possible lines and rejects each until the best fit emerges. Ardizzone then took his students through a path that Sylvia Plath might have followed to produce "Morning Song," a poem about the birth of one of her children. He began with an imaginary series of lines that Plath might have initially written down, recording her general impressions of the birth. Then, rethinking each line in front of the students, he explicitly applied various principles for creating effective poetry (e.g., be concrete) and considered alternate possibilities before picking the one that sounded best. He repeated the mantra "a cousin, a sister," reinforcing the connection between the metaphor from the story and the process of writing a poem. Slowly the actual poem that Plath wrote emerged not as a moment of the instantaneous inspiration of a genius but as the product of systematic labor.

In this magnificent lesson, which may be viewed on the Decoding the Disciplines website, (http://decodingthedisciplines.org/step-3-modeling-mental-operations/) Ardizzone has dealt directly with a major set of bottlenecks in writing. First, and probably most important, he has addressed the inability of many students to understand that writing is a process that requires work, time, and the systematic application of a set of basic principles. Second, even when students have grasped the nature of this process, they may not have the specific intellectual tools that are needed to transform a rough draft into a finished poem. Ardizzone has provided them with a series of particular actions that can be taken to bring about that transformation. Third, he has made it clear that the steps that he is going through in front of his students are the same ones that they can use in their own work. In his elegant use of Nicol's story, Ardizzone has anchored all of this in an easy-to-remember metaphor that can be used throughout a semester to remind students of the need to apply this process to their own efforts to write poems. He needs only to repeat the words "a sister, a cousin" to evoke the entire process. Finally—and this anticipates the material to be covered in chapter 5—Ardizzone has emotionally empowered students to imagine that they themselves could actually do the work of poetry.

In presenting such metaphors, however, it is essential that instructors explicitly link the message contained in the metaphor to the actual operations required in the discipline and, as is so beautifully demonstrated in Ardizzone's lesson, they must allow students to see them actually carry out the operation. The students need to see the cogs turning as the expert performs essential tasks and understand this is the process that they themselves must replicate.

Friederike Neumann and her colleagues at the University of Bielefeld have provided another brilliant example of modeling in a course designed to help first-year students master the skills needed to make use of scholarly works in history. Inspired by both the seminal work of Sam Wineburg (2001) and by decoding, they began by asking students to write down the procedures that they used when they were reading a secondary source in history. Then the students were presented with seven different secondary works in history and asked to choose one. When this was done, a historian, from a field far removed from the material covered in any of these works, entered the room and was presented for the first time with the book the students had chosen. For the next fifteen or twenty minutes the expert demonstrated what he or she would do in the first stages of reading that work, speaking aloud as each step was taken. Thus the students were able to follow the disciplinary patterns of reading as the historian explored the cover, introduction, and conclusion of the work. The class then discussed what they had observed, and wrote about the extent to which their own reading practice did or did not match that of the professional historian. In subsequent weeks these patterns were reinforced in a series of class exercises (Neumann 2015).

The examples of modeling from Ardizzone and Neumann are very elaborate and creative, and they are apt to have a major impact on students' understanding of the respective disciplines. But modeling can also be worked into the teaching process in a less dramatic fashion. Sometimes it may be possible for students to play a role in generating or developing a metaphor. Once a mental operation has been presented, students themselves may be asked to come up with metaphors that capture that way of working, or the implications of the metaphor can be discussed. Often the importance of the mental operations being modeled can be made clear to students by explicitly linking the steps that are being demonstrated to success on exams, papers, or assignments for the course or in later life situations. Yet while it is generally important for the students to at some time actually see the necessary operations being performed and for the instructor to make explicit the role of these steps in the discipline, it is also crucial that the modeling process becomes a central part of the everyday practice of teaching, not just an occasional exercise.

TYPICAL ELEMENTS OF EFFECTIVE MODELING

- Generate a metaphor or analogy that will make the basic operations clear to students.
- Apply the operation that is being modeled to material from the course in front of the students.
- Make explicit the links among the metaphor, the steps being taken by the instructor, and the basic mental operation that is necessary for success in the course.

Making Modeling an Integral Part of a Course

If the operations that underlie a bottleneck were easy for all students, the bottleneck would not exist. When learning is not occurring, there is always something in students' ways of operating in the discipline that does not easily mesh with their preexisting mental strategies, and forming new ways of thinking is generally not easy. It is thus unlikely that a single modeling session will suffice to eliminate the more difficult obstacles to learning. Just repeating the same lesson, however, will be unlikely to produce the kinds of reinforcement that is needed. Therefore, it is necessary to introduce elements of redundancy by modeling the same mental operations in different ways across the semester. As linguists have long noted, languages minimize the possibility of transmission errors in a sentence by conveying information in multiple ways. We must do the same in our teaching, since there is never assurance that a complex pattern will be successfully transmitted in a single pedagogical utterance.

Thus, for new ways of operating to become second nature to students, we must make them a part of the very fabric of the course. The language and organization of the syllabus, the phrasing of instructions on assignments and examples, the nature of team projects, and virtually every other aspect of a course can be used to naturalize the basic ways of thinking in the field. Lectures can be presented not as a distillation of relevant knowledge but as examples of how that knowledge is generated by processes integral to the discipline. If, for example, posing questions and weighing evidence are crucial operations for a course, one can begin a lecture by providing some of the questions one would pose to explore a particular phenomenon and then proceed to considering material that might serve as evidence in the attempt to answer them. The prompts, interventions, and structure of class discussions can further engrain these mental patterns. The combination of all of these efforts with the explicit modeling of basic operations can produce an environment within which students naturally assimilate the epistemology and the procedures of the field and are able to use these to succeed in the course.

The Reemergence of Content

As has been noted throughout this book, decoding requires a major shift of perspective from focusing on what students need to *know* to what they need to *be able to do*. In much traditional teaching one concentrates on the subject matter of the discipline, assuming that the ability to process it is already present in students' minds. In modeling it is necessary to reverse this priority. The instructor must be sure that students are prepared to receive and make use of information before it is transmitted, and crucial ways of thinking, not the content, must determine the structure of a course. A decoded course should be seen primarily as a logical progression of skills development, not just a succession of topics, and this concern should influence every decision in course design and revision.

To soften the sense of loss often produced by this initial shift of attention, it is worth thinking about the consequences of conveying content without also modeling the ways of thinking in the discipline. There is ample evidence that information that is memorized without active intellectual processing is rarely retained for very long. Even more serious is the fact that students can memorize facts without ever really understanding the nature of what they are learning. The consequences of this are particularly visible in biology courses in the United States, where students who have memorized data about evolution for exams sometimes treat what they have learned as the equivalent of religious teachings about creation, without any understanding of the differences in the way that science and religion process the world.

It is also important to focus on mental operations rather than subject matter because, in the practice of most college instructors, content is so powerful that it does not need a champion. Most of us have been so conditioned to prioritize content that it is highly unlikely that the substance of a discipline will ever be completely ignored. But we know that there is a real chance that the steps needed to process that content can be overlooked in teaching because that possibility is being realized in at least some classrooms in virtually every university on the globe.

In this respect, decoding owes a good deal to Grant Wiggins and Jay McTighe's *Understanding by Design* (1998). Their emphasis on focusing on the final outcome of learning underlies much of step 3 (modeling), step 4 (practice), and step 6 (assessment) of the decoding process, just as step 1 (identifying bottlenecks) and step 2 (defining mental operations) can help clarify the goals of anyone applying backward design to a classroom challenge.

The sharing of content does, however, remain a necessity in most courses, and this engenders a tension between the need to provide the details of the subject matter and the necessity of conveying the process of thinking in the discipline. This trade-off is sometimes heightened by the need to add content that may not have been part of the course before decoding. As was mentioned in chapter 2, making explicit the steps required to complete tasks in a course may reveal missing background information that students need to have to complete essential tasks. But the process of deepening one's understanding of crucial mental operations may lead to the inclusion of added content in other ways as well. FLP fellow Richard Durisen, for example, realized that a top-down approach that introduced the findings of astronomers as givens did not actually give students a real understanding of how knowledge was generated in his field. Therefore, he required them to put themselves in the position of nineteenth-century scientists and to make sense out of the data that was available in that period. While these first-year students were not able to fully reconstruct the reasoning process of the earlier astronomers, there was a visible increase in their understanding of the phenomena being studied. Decoding had increased learning, but it has also increased the amount of material that had to be covered (Durisen 2004).

The conflict between covering topics and deepening students' ability to function in the discipline presents a real dilemma, and we need to think seriously about how to meaningfully integrate content with the modeling of basic operations. Sometimes this can be simple. When doing formal modeling, it is generally necessary to be working with real material from the field to show students how experts in the discipline process it. In these cases one can achieve two goals at the same time by focusing on examples that pertain to content that is particularly important. The time devoted to improving skills will thus also increase the likelihood that students learn the material, since a significant amount of class time will be devoted to it. Other possibilities are offered by "flipped" learning, in which time in class is focused on basic skills and information is conveyed elsewhere, most commonly on the internet (Lage, Platt, and Treglia 2000). This possibility can be realized, in part, by creating out-of-class assignments that involve applying crucial mental operations to material read by students on their own. (See chapters 4 and 5.)

Yet, despite these strategies, in most courses there has to be a trade-off between decoding and some of the content previously included. This is often a painful decision to have to make because almost all academics love their subject. There can also be a misplaced sense of responsibility to cover all the topics we ourselves were taught—plus, of course, all the content that has been added since we were undergraduates.

Yet it is becoming increasingly clear that, if we want our students to really learn to think effectively in our disciplines, we must jettison some of the content that we have been burdened with. As Lendol Calder (2006) has argued quite persuasively, our goal should be uncovering the core ways of thinking in our disciplines, not covering them up with masses of facts (see also Bransford, Brown, and Cocking 2000, 20; Sipress and Volker, 2009). Or, as Michael Sweet and Larry Michaelsen have put it, "our challenge is to build courses in which class time can mostly consist of giving students legitimate participation (however peripheral) in the intellectual practices of our disciplines and letting them practice doing so. Covering content is a fundamentally different instructional act from requiring students to use that content" (2012, 10). And, in any case, much of the focus on content rests on a form of magical thinking that assumes that because certain words are uttered in front of a class, something meaningful has happened in the mind of students.

Therefore, like most of the strategies currently being proposed to increase learning, decoding generally requires a reduction in content and the devotion of more time to modeling basic ways of thinking in the discipline. The initial sacrifice of subject matter that we have long considered essential may be initially painful, but those using decoding have generally found that the rewards far outweigh the costs. Teaching students who really understand what they are to do in our courses is ultimately much more satisfying to us and much fairer to those whose learning has been placed in our charge.

Modeling, even at its most effective, is not, however, sufficient. Students must have the opportunity to actively practice the operations that we have taught them. Chapter 4 will be devoted to this crucial step in the decoding process.

4. PRACTICE AND FEEDBACK

DECADES OF RESEARCH and millennia of folk wisdom suggest that learning is not complete and permanent until one has had hands-on experience that puts the new knowledge to work. The very existence of play in a broad range of animals reinforces this notion that true learning always includes an active component. An apprenticeship without practice is unthinkable.

All of this is, of course, a major part of contemporary pedagogy. Virtually no one well versed in the literature about learning today would endorse the old practice of leaving students in the role of passive receiver until the final exam. But the Decoding the Disciplines process can bring a new effectiveness to this aspect of teaching. It can provide crucial insights into what needs to be practiced and how that practice is to be structured.

As we have seen, the first two steps of decoding focus our attention on those areas that are most problematic for students and define with some accuracy the mental operations that students must master to overcome these obstacles. In the process we have also identified those skills that students most need to practice. Here the third and fourth steps are integrally linked. In most situations every operation that has been modeled will be the subject for exercises that will allow students to try out the new ways of functioning and to get some feedback on the extent to which they have succeeded in mastering the new skills. In the process they will have an opportunity to see precisely where their understanding of what needs to be done in the field is incomplete.

To take full advantage of these possibilities, however, it is very important to pay close attention once again to the manner in which the decoding process has broken large, global tasks into their constituent parts. Students get relatively little benefit from exercises that require them to simultaneously mobilize a great variety of skills, many of which they have not fully mastered. A highly complicated undertaking such as writing a paper requires many distinct operations, and none of the needed skills are apt to be greatly strengthened if the student is struggling to perform all of them at once. As my childhood piano teacher taught me, it is very difficult to learn a difficult piece by trying to play it at full speed. Instead, I was taught to first practice each section with one hand, then with the other, sometimes slow and sometimes fast, until each of the complex schemas required for mastery of the whole was in place and could be synthesized into a full interpretation of the music. Only then could the complete composition be performed with confidence. There is no reason to suppose that learning to perform thinking in a discipline should be any different, and decoding provides a clear way to bring this kind of practice to the learning of an academic discipline. It focuses attention on the places where practice is needed and breaks the large tasks into discrete operations. When these operations prove difficult, it becomes clear to the student and the instructor where more work is needed. When mastery has been attained, the progress is quite visible, and all parties know that it is time to move on to the next challenge.

Strategies for Allowing Students to Practice Key Mental Operations

In the practice step, as in modeling, backward design is essential (Wiggins and McTighe 1998). One must avoid the temptation of becoming too enamored by the specific technique that is being employed in the exercise. Instead, attention should remain focused on the outcome of instilling in students' minds the mental patterns that are required for successful work in the discipline. At all times instructors must keep their eyes on that prize. But when this goal is clear, the vast possibilities offered by contemporary pedagogy take on a new meaning. Like the bride groom in Tony Ardizzone's modeling lesson described in chapter 3, the instructor can wait as different possibilities are presented—collaborative learning, problem-based learning, team-based learning, and the like—until the perfect match appears.

The earlier steps of decoding have prepared the way, but there are still a few basic principles that must be kept in mind. First, as noted above, it is important to initially keep the various operations distinct. If too many different ways of operating are practiced at the same time, there is a danger that none of them may be sufficiently reinforced or that students will become overwhelmed.

Second, it is important to reinforce the learning repeatedly. It takes time to assimilate complex operations, and if they are not firmly rooted in the minds of students, they will soon disappear. Thus it is important to return to the modeling and practice of a particular operation multiple times across the course. This requires some creativity, since simply repeating the same exercise may have little added effect. Instead, one must provide different types of practice, all of which reinforce the same patterns. And practice in different media can be coordinated—for example, the work in online exercises can be strengthened by in-class team exercises that involve the same operations.

Third, it is important to think strategically about the order in which practice is presented. Typically, it is best to begin with the simplest operations and then move on to those that are more complex. Those mental operations that are more demanding or more essential for operating in the discipline should receive more attention than those that are easier to master or less essential. And, of course, modeling and practice need to be coordinated.

Typically the instructor models the processes and then gives students opportunities to practice them. Occasionally, however, it may be desirable to reverse the process so that students begin with a sense of the problem and with the context within which experts generate their knowledge. In a memorable practice lesson, geologist Jim Brophy divided the other instructors in his Indiana University Freshman Learning Project (FLP) cohort into learning teams, placed five rocks in front of each, and then asked the groups to determine everything they could figure out about the objects' origins based on their appearances. Building on some of the responses and explaining the fallacy of others, Brophy was then able to model ways of operating as a geologist, at the same time that he drew the group into the thought processes that generate geological knowledge. Having already struggled with trying to understand this phenomenon, the group was much more emotionally invested in finding out the solution.

Content is such a powerful force for most academic experts that it is generally best to initially set it aside and work out the sequence of modeling and practice, adding the subject matter later. Sometimes, however, particular elements of content lend themselves so well to practicing specific operations that including them in the planning of practice will help shape the order in which the skills are sequenced.

When thinking strategically it is also important to consider the amalgamation of basic operations into more complex skills. As has been noted repeatedly, one of the great advantages of step 2 of the decoding process (defining mental operations) is the manner in which it breaks up the thinking tasks of a field. But it is still necessary to lead students to more complex tasks that involve the coordination of multiple operations. Therefore, it is often important to follow the modeling and practicing of specific operations with exercises in which students must integrate these into more complex tasks. It is, for example, inappropriate to assign a paper early in the semester if large numbers of students begin the course without an understanding of the steps required to accomplish this task. It is necessary first to model operations, such as the creation of a thesis, the use of evidence, and the consideration of counterarguments. But once these skills have been presented and they are fixed in students' minds through repeated practice, it is possible to begin to give them more complicated assignments that involve the integration of several operations and, finally, to move on actually assigning papers.

Finally, a crucial part of this process of treating practice consciously and strategically is to make its purpose clear to students themselves. Many students arrive in college after a dozen years of endless assignments without any notion of why they have been doing such labor. If practice is to be maximally effective, they need to understand that it has a purpose and that it is in their benefit to use it. This can be achieved by making the decoding process transparent for students and by explicitly linking the process of practicing basic mental operations to their success in the course and beyond. This connection can be made explicit in the wording of the exercise itself.

Students often express their awareness of the usefulness of the practice in decoded courses. At the end of one seminar, for example, students were asked to write anonymous advice on succeeding in the course for those taking it in the future. The use of the decoding process had led to the creation of weekly assignments, designed to give students practice at specific mental operations that were crucial to the discipline at hand. It might have been expected that some resentment might have been expressed about the work that this entailed. Instead, half of the fourteen respondents chose spontaneously to focus on the positive impact of this aspect of the course on student success, with comments such as, "Spend time on your homework assignment. A bit of effort on each weekly response can save an incredible amount of time when you're writing your paper," or, "Do the online assignments and spend some quality time on it. It will help you out in several ways and even has future benefits." These and other bits of advice have been made available to those taking later iterations of the course, thus reinforcing the metarealization that these assignments were actually part of a rational system in which they were systematically being set up for future success.

To gain full advantage from decoded practice and feedback, however, students must be able to view such assignments as part of a process leading to mastery rather than as a series of judgments about their worthiness to be in college. As John Bransford and his colleagues have pointed out, "an unwritten norm that operates in some classrooms is never to get caught making a mistake or not knowing an answer" (Bransford, Brown, and Cocking 2000, 145). This has often been reinforced by college testing practices in which a single final exam determines much of the grade. This kind of culture has led many students to view all mistakes as disasters that must be avoided at all costs—an expectation that can be very detrimental to learning, since the willingness to make and learn from mistakes is a key mental operation required in virtually any intellectual undertaking. The negative impact of such expectations can be lessened by building into the course opportunities for making useful, "low-cost" mistakes—that is, occasions that allow students to receive information about what basic skills they have or have not mastered without disastrous consequences.

But it may also be necessary for instructors to treat students' attitude toward success and failure as a bottleneck to learning worth decoding. This would involve systematically considering what experts in this particular discipline do when they encounter difficulties. Then it would be useful to explicitly model for students specific responses to mistakes and the more general attitude of experts in the field toward learning from errors.

STRATEGIC CONCERNS FOR CREATING OPPORTUNITIES FOR PRACTICE

- Be sure to base practice on operations essential for overcoming common bottlenecks.
- Begin by giving students practice on individual operations rather than on complex tasks that require multiple operations.
- Have students practice basic operations multiple times and in different forms.
- Arrange practice in a logical order, integrating it with modeling and moving from simpler to more complex operations.
- When appropriate, provide students with opportunities to integrate simple operations into more complex tasks.
- Provide students with opportunities to make useful mistakes at minimal cost.
- Help students understand the reason for the practice.

Developing shared metaphors for this process would also be useful to give it more traction. For those students who are gamers, there is a ready metaphor available to help them make this mental shift, since almost all computer games model this process of learning through mistakes. Others may have been exposed as children to Joanna Cole and Bruce Degan's marvelous Magic School Bus series and can be reminded of Ms. Frizzle's maxim, "Take chances, make mistakes, get messy!" But whatever the route into students' consciousness, it is very often useful to be sure that they understand that one of the essential mental operations in all disciplines is the willingness to experiment, make mistakes, and learn from them.

Creating Effective Opportunities for Practice

Within the context of the strategic concerns presented above, almost any aspect of a course can provide the occasion for practice. It can occur in class or outside it, and can be individual or team based. It can take traditional forms such as essays or problem sets, or it can involve the creation of quite new types of work. But whatever the nature of the activity, practice must serve to reinforce specific operations and must be repeated often enough for these ways of acting to become second nature.

In many cases this involves refocusing existing assignments more explicitly on the specific bottlenecks that are impeding learning. If students are able to do basic calculations in a math class but encounter a bottleneck when they need to transfer these skills to a different type of problem, simply giving them more problem sets will not in itself solve the difficulty. Instead they can be presented with two different problems and asked to explain whether both can be solved using the same approach, and then asked to provide the reason for their decision. Thus, practice will be focused on the precise mental operations that are problematic (Bransford et al. 2000, 142).

Jill Robinson, an FLP fellow from Indiana University's Department of Chemistry, became aware through the decoding process that an essential bottleneck in her courses was the fact that many of her students were trying to memorize answers rather than solve problems. Traditional assignments in the field only reinforced this misunderstanding of the discipline. Therefore, after modeling problem-solving strategies in chemistry, she began adding questions in which students were asked not simply for an answer but instead for a plan for arriving at an answer.

In instructional design courses many students encounter a bottleneck when they are asked to put the skills they have learned to work responding to the needs of particular clients. Therefore, instead of simply giving them a series of separate problems to solve, an instructor might give them two hypothetical clients and require the students to explain how and why they would make different suggestions to each.

If students in a history course have difficulty systematically defending an interpretation in an essay, simply assigning additional papers will not necessarily eliminate this bottleneck. After having analyzed the steps that experts in the field use to support an interpretation (step 2) and modeled each of these for students (step 3), the instructor might create a scaffold of assignments that would allow students to practice some of the basic operations required for this task. In one of my own courses, steps such as these were employed across the semester:

1. Students were presented with an interpretation and asked to make a list of the points that they would need to defend to make that interpretation credible to their readers.
2. Next they were asked to take several of these points and identify a piece of evidence that could be used to support each.
3. They then wrote a sentence or two from a hypothetical paper that would explain why a particular piece of evidence made the given interpretation more credible.
4. Next the students generated an alternative interpretation of the phenomenon and explained what they would need to do to demonstrate that one view was more convincing than the other.
5. Finally, after exercises like these had made many of the basic operations required for writing papers second nature, the students were asked to integrate these operations in an actual paper.

It might be objected that such a process is too time-consuming for the instructor. In some cases that may be accurate, and thus it will be necessary to pursue other strategies. But it should be noted that reading each student's response to steps 1–4 can be done in a matter of seconds and, if papers are going to be assigned anyway, the process of actually grading them will be both faster and more pleasant after students have had a little practice at some of the steps necessary for producing readable work.

The process of generating occasions for focused practice can also be greatly facilitated by considering how other instructors have responded to this challenge. In addition to the examples in this work and in Joan Middendorf and Leah Shopkow's forthcoming *Decoding the Disciplines: How to Help Students Learn Critical Thinking,* a section of the Decoding the Disciplines website (http://decodingthe disciplines.org/step-4-creating-opportunities-for-students-to-practice-essential -mental-operations/) is devoted to practice exercises, using this approach in a number of disciplines. Readers are encouraged to view these examples and to consider adding materials from their own courses.

It is also important to remember that, as in the identification of key mental operations, the existing literature on the scholarship of teaching and learning can make the process of providing practice easier. There exist great models for this step that can be readily adapted to decoding. The kind of exercises presented in great profusion in Gerald Graff and Cathy Birkenstein's *They Say/I Say* (2006) can, for example, easily be adapted to give students practice at a great variety of basic mental operations. And this is only a single example of the hundreds of existing models for creating decoding practice that are waiting for us in the existing literature on the scholarship of teaching and learning.

Combining Decoding with Active Learning Techniques

Decoding is a framework within which to plan teaching and learning, rather than a specific teaching technique, and as such it can be combined effectively with many practical approaches to increasing learning. As must be apparent from the examples above, decoding is so compatible with collaborative learning that it is difficult to imagine using it without group activities. To combine the two an instructor must simply focus the activities of learning teams on providing opportunities to practice the mental operations that are crucial at a particular moment in the course. The process of breaking down global processes into their component parts actually makes the creation of group tasks much simpler, and interactions within the group can greatly facilitate the assimilation of new ways of operating within the discipline. Collaborative techniques also allow an instructor to provide many more occasions for practice, since group work can often be ungraded or, when grades are assigned, the total number to be evaluated is greatly reduced.

The Just-in-Time Teaching (JiTT) exercises developed by Gregor Novak and his colleagues also provide a particularly effective tool for decoding practice. In their original JiTT model they created practice exercises (warm-ups and puzzles) targeting particular issues that often prove problematic for students in physics classes (Novak et al. 1999). These not only allowed students to make an attempt at solving problems online before class but also gave instructors the information needed to focus class time on those issues that are most problematic for students. Selected results of the preclass work provided the subject matter for interactive in-class work that increased student involvement. More recently, this approach has been applied to a much wider range of disciplines with very positive results (Novak 2011; Simkins and Maier 2010). The decoding process can help instructors using JiTT to focus on those mental operations that are most essential in a course, and the preclass exercises and in-class discussions provide a perfect vehicle for decoding modeling and practice, since it is possible to focus very specifically on particular mental operations.[1]

Arlene Díaz has demonstrated that decoding can also be used very effectively in conjunction with team-based learning (TBL; see Shopkow, Díaz, Middendorf, and Pace 2013). As described by Larry Michaelsen and Michael Sweet (2012), TBL, like JiTT, moves much of the responsibility for learning onto the students themselves, albeit within a well-structured and supportive environment. Students are expected to carefully cover a set of readings on their own outside of class. When they arrive in class they are then presented with a short multiple-choice test, which each student first takes on his or own; then the test is taken again in learning teams. The group test is structured so that the students receive immediate feedback on correct answers, and teams can submit appeals, arguing that answers that had been judged incorrect could, in fact, be seen as right. The instructor then clarifies any points that the teams have been unable to master on their own. This pedagogical structure provides an excellent framework for offering students opportunities to practice mental operations identified through the decoding process.

These brief descriptions of JiTT and TBL do not, of course, begin to do justice to pedagogical strategies that are the result of deep thinking about teaching and learning and that develop intricate processes for implementing the resulting insights. Both succeed in shifting more of the responsibility of learning to the students, and both create spaces in which students are actively engaging in the practice of the discipline. As Sweet and Michaelsen note, "As students evaluate the cases and argue the merits of one choice over another, teachers often report that students aren't talking about history or about literature or about anthropology. They are *talking history* and *talking literature* and *talking anthropology*" (2012, p. 26, emphasis in the original).

But to be maximally effective these conversations must help students get past those obstacles to learning that most often create difficulties, and it is here that decoding can come into play. By clearly identifying bottlenecks and exploring the mental operations that are required for mastery of the discipline, it can help instructors focus their use of JiTT or TBL on precisely those points where this kind of intense work is needed most. In addition, decoding can provide useful ideas for modeling those mental operations that the student teams have the most difficulty mastering on their own.

Much the same might be said about many of the other approaches to teaching and learning that now offer such rich alternatives to traditional pedagogy. Problem-based learning can be made more effective through application of decoding's find-the-bottleneck, define-the-operations, model-the-process sequence (steps 1–3). A variety of approaches to teaching writing could be strengthened by more explicit analysis of bottlenecks and the mental operations that must be mastered to overcome them. But regardless of the approach that is ultimately chosen as most appropriate for a particular situation, decoding can give instructors a clearer vision of how the technique can be used most effectively to overcome obstacles to student learning.

Providing Feedback

One of the main drawbacks of many traditional tests and assignments is that they often leave students with little useful information about what they have successfully mastered and what they still need to work on. A low letter grade on a paper or exam tells students that there is a problem, but it provides almost no information about the nature of that problem or what needs to be done to correct it. This situation is made even worse when this limited response arrives late in the course.

In the practice step, decoding seeks to remedy this situation by giving students useful information about their mastery of specific mental operations at every stage of the course. The forms of practice described in this chapter set the stage for this kind of regular, focused feedback; they can allow the development of students' metacognitive knowledge about their own progress through the discipline and greatly facilitate learning.

This process is so crucial to learning that it is worth investing thought in finding ways to maximize the flow of information to students about their performance. When considerations of time and teaching load allow it, comments on student work should be quite explicit about which mental operations students have mastered and which still require work. But even when the opportunities for such individualized responses are limited, strategies exist for sharing this information with students. In creating a multiple choice test or an online assignment, it is often possible to design items that assess the presence or absence of certain steps in disciplinary practice. This information can be made available when the exams are returned so that students can determine where more work is needed and common mistakes can be discussed generically in class. An even more effective method for delivering feedback on mastery of specific operations is provided by going over examples of student work in class, using the JiTT process described above.

But it is often useful to explicitly facilitate the development of such self-knowledge by creating occasions for students to create a mental map of their own mastery of the discipline. After students undertake a major project, they can be provided with a checklist asking them to consider whether they actually did essential operations. They can be asked to review a series of their own assignments and to write a self-evaluation of their strengths and the areas in which more work is needed. Critiquing others' work can also provide a moment in which students can gain a greater awareness of their own progress.

Strategic Considerations in Creating Opportunities for Practice

In designing occasions for practice, as in all aspects of teaching, it is important to think strategically. The time and resources available for instruction are always limited, and it is important to make careful and conscious decisions about how they are invested. Thus a crucial consideration in creating opportunities for practice is the amount of time required of both the instructor and the students. The need for repeated occasions for practice can become a serious drain on the time and energies of all parties; this is an important consideration that should not be ignored in an attempt to do everything possible to increase student learning. Teaching seriously is a marathon, not a hundred-yard dash, and it is important to find ways to conserve our energy for the long haul. Therefore it is important that at least some of the practice required for decoding be exempt from grading or from excess work for the students outside class.

It is now well established that students cannot concentrate on a lecture more than fifteen to twenty minutes at most and that, if one chooses to use this form of teaching, it is necessary to add "change-up" exercises to reset students' attention (Middendorf and Kalish 1996). This can provide a perfect occasion for individual or group practice of an operation relevant to the subject of the lecture. Building on the examples above, one might interrupt a lecture in chemistry with a challenge for students to devise a particularly effective way to solve a problem that arises from the subject matter being considered. A presentation in computer science could be punctuated with opportunities to consider alternate strategies for debugging a particular type of program. Electronic clickers can play a very effective role by allowing instant feedback in class about what mental operation students have or have not mastered.

Discussion is already a part of many courses, and there is no reason why some of the time devoted to this may not be used to strengthen students' grasp of particular operations. If, for example, many students are having trouble identifying appropriate evidence to support their interpretations, it is possible to stop a discussion at crucial points and have different groups compete to find a particularly effective example to support or to oppose a specific position. If the task of integrating details into a coherent argument is a challenge for many students, the

THE STRATEGIC USE OF PRACTICE

Carefully structured practice
- reinforces basic mental operations
- gives students practice at these tasks
- gives them a clear picture of how to combine these skills in larger, more complex undertakings
- makes clear how this work is of benefit to students
- focuses on important content
- provides information that is useful in assessing progress

instructor could end a discussion with a request that teams generate topic sentences for imaginary papers on the issue that has been discussed. And a discussion can be framed in ways that make the epistemological configurations of the discipline explicit by posing a problem for the group and asking the class to consider the grounds on which arguments may be constructed within the field.

Whatever form of practice an instructor chooses to employ in a particular course, it is essential to see such exercises as part of a seamless series of decoding steps. Building on the identification of the most serious bottlenecks (step 1), the definition of essential disciplinary operations needed to overcome these problems (step 2), and careful modeling of these essential skills (step 3), strategic practice can allow students to internalize these ways of operating (step 4). As we shall see in chapter 6, this leads the way to more useful assessment of learning. But the success of all these steps assumes a certain level of commitment on the part of the students and the absence of emotional blocks that keep students from engaging with the material. As any experienced teacher knows, these preconditions for learning are not always present. Therefore, in chapter 5 we will move to step 5, dealing with motivational bottlenecks.

5. MOTIVATION AND EMOTIONAL BOTTLENECKS

THUS FAR WE have been dealing primarily with cognitive bottlenecks—that is, problems that result from the intellectual challenge of adapting to the mental patterns of a discipline. But emotional issues can also frustrate learning. Operating successfully in a decoded class requires a certain level of student motivation, and without that energy it is unlikely that modeling and practice will be entirely successful. Moreover, even when students are willing to invest in a course there may be negative emotional reactions to the way it is taught or to its subject matter that interfere with learning.

As we shall see, the very nature of the Decoding the Disciplines process tends to automatically lessen some of these problems. But it is also necessary to strive to increase students' commitment to their work and to develop strategies for dealing with dysfunctional emotions before they disrupt the learning process. In some cases this involves borrowing strategies from other approaches, and in others the decoding process itself can provide ways to minimize the impact of these problems. Such responses are, however, only possible after one has identified the nature of the difficulty and systematically developed a strategy for dealing with it.

Before launching this discussion of the emotional dimensions of decoding, it is necessary to note that in this section I am particularly indebted to my colleagues Joan Middendorf, Arlene Díaz, and Leah Shopkow. I had previously done some exploration in the area of teaching emotionally charged topics, but much of what follows in this chapter would probably have never come into being without their ideas and inspiration. Joan first recognized that the focus on students' preconceptions, being used to explain cognitive resistance to new concepts in areas like physics and biology, could also be a very useful tool in exploring emotional resistance; Arlene and Leah were particularly effective in linking general concerns about emotional bottlenecks to specific strategies for overcoming them. Their ideas have allowed us to add an emotional dimension to our earlier explorations of the origins of cognitive obstacles to learning.

Motivation

There is a natural and quite understandable tendency for human beings to avoid humiliation, and the school experience of many students has been a history of systematic shaming. They have been judged and found wanting so many times that they can guess the verdict before they even enter the classroom. Such negative judgments can be the result of a natural difficulty in certain areas of learning, racial, ethnic, or class prejudice, inequality of educational opportunity, or simply the bad luck of encountering ineffective teaching during K–12 education. Regardless of the cause, the result is almost always a withdrawal from the learning process. It is less painful to receive negative evaluations if one has not really tried, and it is rare for students to continue to pour energy into courses if they are convinced that success is beyond their reach.

Therefore, a key element in any effort to draw such students into the learning process must be to create the impression that this time things might be different, that this time work might actually bring rewards. The very nature of decoding makes this more likely. By breaking learning operations down into their component parts and then systematically modeling each, we make it easier for students to imagine success. As was suggested by one instructor we worked with, we need to feed students small victories until they "get hooked"; then we can begin to up the ante.

It is important to stress that this does not represent a "dumbing down" of the learning process. We expect students to go as far or farther than in our pre-Decoding classes. But now more students can see a route to success and, therefore, make a commitment to get there.

Students' sense that they are operating in a rational universe in which success is possible may also contribute to removing a second obstacle to motivation: the notion that the instructor is the enemy. Adolescents often experience high school as if they were prisoners of war, unable to regain their freedom, but dedicated to cooperating as little as possible with their captors. Those students who enter college directly from secondary school often bring these attitudes with them, and this mind-set is reinforced by courses in which the instructions seem unintelligible and the tasks impossible. Decoding can often contribute to resetting these emotional expectations. When the efforts of the instructor to help the students succeed are obvious, the image of prison guard can often be replaced with that of coach.

Yet while decoding can automatically make a contribution to increasing motivation, it is often necessary to think systematically about how to amplify this effect. In our work with the History Learning Project (HLP), we have focused on two areas. First we consciously reshaped assignments to break students' negative patterns of expectations. Second we used the power of social learning and public accountability to motivate students to make a greater commitment to the work of the course.

In the first area we were influenced by the work of Bob Bain (Bain 2006; Shopkow 2013a). Building on the ideas of Erving Goffman, David Olson, and others, Bain argues that certain patterns of passivity have been so engrained in students through years of traditional textbooks and teaching methods that these ways of operating have become automatic. To induce students to engage more actively, it is necessary to consciously interrupt these classroom rituals in ways that fundamentally alter their expectations about their role in the class.

Therefore, we consciously set out to replace familiar classroom activities or assignments that automatically evoke unconscious patterns of passivity and non-involvement. On the very first day of each HLP course, we created active learning situations in which students were required to make choices and to interact with others. We created syllabi that are strikingly different from those that students are accustomed to. And we built on a generation of work in active learning to present students each day with nontraditional tasks.

The area in which learning is most ritualized and automatic, however, is that of assignments and testing. The very form of many traditional assessments often automatically prompts students to revert to passive patterns of reaction that maximize rote memorization and minimize engagement and critical thinking. As we have seen in chapter 4, decoding in itself calls for the creation of new forms of practice that zero in on specific operations, and as we shall see in chapter 6, this need for specificity also fosters experimentation in assessments. These changes, which flow naturally from the decoding project, can have the positive secondary effect of reshaping student expectations. The unexpected can, of course, be disquieting to those accustomed to traditional forms of assignments and testing, and it is necessary to explain the advantages of the new approaches to students. But such changes can help hit the reset button in students' heads and encourage them to consider abandoning old patterns of passivity and minimal involvement in the course.

We have also found that making students' effort public increased the energy that they put into our courses. Students are very often much more sensitive to the negative judgments of their peers than they are to those of instructors. When they know that their work—or the lack thereof—will be seen by an entire class or even a larger audience, they have an extra incentive to become involved in the activities of the course.

Like interrupting classroom rituals, making students' work public is very compatible with the other elements of decoding. As we have seen, it is generally advisable to conduct a good deal of the practice of basic mental operations through team assignments. If the tasks assigned to these teams are carefully designed, they can provide an occasion in which the level of work that students have put into the course is made visible. For example, some of the exercises that give students practice at basic operations can also require them to cover a certain portion of the reading. This work can be brought to class and serve as the basis of a team project that will be graded. When students know that the assignment that they are doing at home will be passed to other members of a learning team in class and thus provide part of the foundation for a collective project, they are much more likely to be concerned about the quality of their work.

Competition among teams can also be used as a motivator, if their work is made visible in the form of presentations, posters, or websites. Team members will often pressure their less-involved colleagues to make a greater commitment to their work in order to avoid the public shame of work that is visibly inferior to that of other groups. The impact of this was corroborated as part of a very interesting study of the uses of data mining to gain information about student work in history courses by Ali Erkan and Michael Smith at Ithaca College. In a U.S. history survey each student team was assigned a topic (e.g., race relations, immigration) and asked to create a shared blog on which they followed that issue throughout the time span covered by the course. Each student team was unable to see the blogs of the other teams, but Smith and Erkan were able to get a measure of the effort of each group simply by counting the number of links created each week. Early in the semester the increase in links of all the teams was slow, but at a certain point some of the teams had bursts of energy that rapidly expanded their blogs, while others continued to advance at the same slow rate. When in November all of the blogs were made available to the entire class, those groups that had lagged behind suddenly threw themselves into the work and showed rapid improvement (Smith and Erkan 2009).[1]

This kind of incentive can often be increased if the products of the teams are made visible to an even larger audience. Arlene Díaz and Leah Shopkow have played a particularly key role in developing the goals described above and in creating effective means of achieving them. They have transformed their classes' final presentations into public performances in which each team is judged by outside experts who comment on the work and award prizes. Leah has gone a step further and placed the team posters in public locations on campus, where students know that their work will be seen by hundreds or even thousands of others (Shopkow et al. 2013a) The impact of this approach can be strengthened even more when the work is part of a service learning course in which students see the concrete use of their work.

At this point the two motivational strategies we have stressed—interrupting rituals and making work visible—merge and reinforce one another. At the core of most students' educational history has been the ritual of preparing work, submitting it to the instructor, receiving grades and (sometimes) comments, and then throwing the paper or assignment away. They have been conditioned to think of the work as a meaningless act that is only done to prevent the negative consequences posed by a disappointed authority figure. When their work is part of a larger activity, when it is shared and evaluated publically, and—especially— when it is put to some use beyond the classroom, an entire set of expectations about what schoolwork means can be dispelled; it then begins to take on many of the qualities that mark most forms of professional activity, and this experience can be transformative for many students. (See, for example, Erekson 2011.)

Emotional Bottlenecks

Such motivational strategies, combined with the relative ease with which students move through levels of learning in decoded courses, can greatly increase the energy that they invest. But there are other emotional issues that can interfere with learning—affective bottlenecks that are the equivalent to the cognitive bottlenecks that we have considered in earlier chapters. If these obstacles are not systematically addressed, it is unlikely that the process described above will be entirely successful. Instead, sullen withdrawal or angry eruptions will block the learning process for many students, and they will be unlikely to master the basic operations they need for success in the course and later in their lives.

In working with such emotional bottlenecks we have found it useful to rely on three principles. First, it is generally a mistake to wait until emotional issues appear in a course to begin to deal with them. By the time a student has begun to openly display negative emotions, these patterns of feeling and thinking may have been so deeply engrained that they may be impossible to alter. Therefore, if there are predictable patterns of emotional resistance or places in a course that evoke dysfunctional emotional responses, it is best to prepare for them in advance. In many cases strategies for minimizing emotional bottlenecks should be in place before students arrive on the first day of class (Pace 2003).

Second, much of our work rests on the assumption that cognitive and affective issues are closely connected. The way that one reacts to some idea or event in the world is linked to the manner in which the mind organizes the experience intellectually. Behind students' negative reactions to the way a course is being taught or to its content there are certain cognitive assumptions about what is supposed to happen in a college class or about the subject matter. We have found that it is often simpler to address such problems on an intellectual level rather than to engage emotions directly. This is not to say that there is no place for emotions in the classroom. There are undoubtedly times when students' emotions should be dealt with directly and explicitly. But many of the negative emotions that surface in college courses are entirely dysfunctional, and, if they can be prevented by interventions on the intellectual plane, so much the better (Cameron-Bandler and Lebeau 1986).

Third, we have found that most affective obstacles to learning are linked to preconceptions that students bring to the course. In some cases these preconceptions involve students' understanding of the nature of work in the discipline. Students encounter these *procedural bottlenecks* because they already have ideas about what is supposed to happen in a discipline and are upset when what they

---

PRINCIPLES FOR DEALING WITH
EMOTIONAL BOTTLENECKS

- It is generally better to deal with dysfunctional emotions before they manifest themselves as a visible problem.
- Feelings are always connected to cognitive operations, and it is often easier to address affective issues by changing the intellectual processes that generate dysfunctional emotions.
- Emotional bottlenecks generally result from a mismatch between what is actually encountered in a course and the preconceptions of students about the ways of operating in the field or its content.

---

actually have to do in a course does not match these expectations. In other situations the emotional friction arises from a mismatch between students' preexisting beliefs about the content of a course and the ideas about that material that they encounter across the term. Such *narrative bottlenecks* generally arise when the ideas that emerge in a course seem to be in conflict with what they already believe about the world. But in either case, the apparent contradiction between student expectations and the reality of the course must be resolved before learning can occur smoothly.

These three principles can work together effectively to prevent much of the emotional damage that occurs in many courses. Working backward, it is possible to begin early in the course to identify students' preconceptions about the field or its content. As Lee Shulman has written, "To take *learning* seriously, we need to take *learners* seriously" (1999, 2), and this involves devoting energy to reconstructing those parts of the students' visions of the world that are directly relevant to the course that we are teaching. Possible conflicts between these beliefs and what students will actually encounter in the course can be considered, and plans can be developed to reshape students' cognitive approach before such ways of understanding the field or its content can interrupt learning. While such an approach cannot, of course, eliminate all the dysfunctional emotions that appear in teaching, it can eliminate much of the affective noise that gets in the way of learning. Therefore, the rest of this chapter will explore responses to such emotional bottlenecks.

Procedural Bottlenecks

As educational theorists from Jean Piaget to William Perry to the proponents of threshold concepts have argued, there can be a natural resistance to conceptual change. In the original language of Piaget, to maintain its internal integrity an organism must maintain a balance between assimilating information within existing structures and accommodating those structures to new ways of organizing its relationship to the world. Learning something new almost always involves giving up some internal schema that has helped the organism function in the past, and every living creature must set limits on how much fundamental change it allows at any particular moment (Piaget 1952; see also Perry 1970; Timmermans 2010). Moreover, every living thing inhabits a world in which energy resources are limited; and change, whether physical or mental, almost always involves the expenditure of great amounts of effort.

This natural conservatism, which Piaget suggests begins at conception, has now been widely recognized as a contributing factor to student learning difficulties. This self-preservation mechanism can be activated when the procedures or worldview that students encounter in a college class seem to negate those that have functioned for them in the past. In fields like physics a great deal of work has been done exploring the ways in which learning is blocked by the mismatch between students' preexisting ways of dealing with the world and the material they are being taught in college. (See, for example, Bransford, Brown, and Cocking 2000; Chi 2008.) Most of this work, however, has focused primarily on the cognitive problems generated by this process. The HLP, led in this area by Joan Middendorf, has explored the emotional dimensions of this collision between precollege notions and what is actually encountered at the university level.

When students feel that what they are being asked to learn requires them to abandon ways of operating that have worked in the past and to expend great amounts of mental energy on new, untested mental schemas, the result can be emotional bottlenecks to learning which can be every bit as serious as the more narrowly cognitive bottlenecks that we have encountered in earlier chapters. In this section I will consider those obstacles to learning that result from a mismatch between students' notions of what they expect to do in particular disciplines and what really works in college courses in these fields. Later I will turn to those emotional bottlenecks that result from the collision of students' preexisting conceptions of the world with the ideas that they encounter at the university level.

Students enter higher education with ideas about what is required for academic success. Sometimes this preconception is based on their actual experience in high school courses. In other times it derives from general cultural stereotypes about the nature of specific types of intellectual work. Problems arise when these conceptions of what works are at odds with what must actually be done to succeed in a particular discipline. And at the core of this conflict is almost always a fundamental misunderstanding of the epistemology of the field. Students are attempting to perform in one "knowledge game" when a very different set of rules are actually at play.

Certain misconceptions about the nature of work appear in many disciplines. Thus, students commonly expect to succeed through rote memorization in classes where analysis or interpretation are required. They often imagine that mechanically doing "plug-and-chug" mathematical calculations will resolve all problems, when analysis is actually what is called for. And, as we have seen, they may be waiting for a simple, objective answer to questions that cannot be resolved so simply.

When there is a great difference between students' conception of work in the field and the procedures that are actually required, cognitive dissonance can produce an emotional reaction that threatens to derail learning. One has only to put oneself in the position of students making this mistake to understand how strong, negative feelings can be generated by such a mismatch. They have signed up for a course expecting that a certain kind of work would be necessary. In many cases the prior notion of what it means to study in a particular field has been reinforced by positive rewards in high school courses in the same field. Now, in college, these students find that their instructor is operating under an entirely different set of rules. Suddenly work that might have been praised in their high school course is receiving low grades. Course activities have nothing to do with the field as the students understand it. The students have fallen through a disciplinary rabbit hole.

All of this is made more emotionally explosive by the fact that most students do not understand what is happening. As Sam Wineburg (2001) has pointed out, high school text books tend to be written in a generic style in which all disciplinary knowledge is presented in much the same form. In college this lingua franca is replaced with a babel of different disciplinary languages that can be bewildering to students. This is particularly serious in educational systems, such as those in the United States, where students are commonly asked to inhabit radically different intellectual universes in a single day. But even in other systems, students entering college are generally required to drastically alter their ways of operating on the basis of a few—largely implicit—clues about how college differs from high school.

Thus, as David Bartholomae brilliantly put it in a classic essay, "Every time a student sits down to write for us, he has to invent the university for the occasion— invent the university, that is, or a branch of it, like History or Economics or English" (Bartholomae 1986, 4). Not surprisingly, this act of invention often goes awry, and students make quite incorrect assumptions about what is expected of them. Colleges and universities rarely minimize this confusion by providing a clear conceptual map of what happens in higher education. Thus, students very often find themselves in a world in which strategies that once worked are now quite inadequate, and they have little or no understanding of what is happening to them.

There are two common, negative responses to this situation. Students can become convinced that they are simply inadequate for the task and withdraw— emotionally, but often physically, as well. When they do remain in the class, such students respond passively, putting as little as possible into the course. Some blame their teacher and seethe with anger about why the subject is not being taught in the "right" manner. They may wait silently for an instructor who really knows how to teach the subject "correctly," or they might express their annoyance openly, challenging grades or trying to rally other students to their negative views of the instructor. But whether their reaction is expressed in withdrawal or anger, learning is obstructed.

Minimizing the Negative Emotional Impact of Procedural Bottlenecks

Before we can begin to neutralize the emotional impact of these procedural bottlenecks, we need to know what they are. In many cases they will eventually be revealed in the practice that decoding requires of students. Since these exercises or activities are focused on particular mental operations, student mistakes will provide us with indirect information about how they believe they should operate in the discipline. But, as has been noted above, one of our principles for responding to emotional bottlenecks is to intervene before the cognitive misunderstanding has generated emotional problems.

Therefore, it is often useful to develop an exercise to determine students' strategies for success in the discipline at the very beginning of a course. If students are likely to have already taken a class in the field, they may be asked to write briefly about what they liked most and least about the work they encountered. They can also be presented with four or five kinds of activities and asked which most resembles work in this discipline. They can be given examples of the kinds of problems typically dealt with in the field and asked not to solve them but instead to describe the steps they would take to respond to this challenge. Or, as Leah Shopkow has suggested, one can ask a more specific question, such as, "Besides hard work, what would someone have to do to be successful in this course?" (Middendorf et al. 2015).

Once typical misunderstandings of the disciplines have been identified, an instructor may treat these problems much like the cognitive bottlenecks discussed earlier. It is necessary to make explicit the ways that experts function in these areas and then to model and give practice on these operations. Given the emotional charge that is linked to particular preconceptions about the discipline, however, it may be important to take extra steps to assure that students remain on board with the learning process.

This generally requires helping students understand the rationale behind the processes that are used in the field. It is always important to remember the ways of operating that the students bring to the course probably seemed functional in earlier contexts—and in some cases may have actually been effective in high school classes. Asking them to completely abandon these schemas simply on the word of the stranger at the front of the classroom may not produce real change. In many cases the call for new ways of approaching the subject will generate less resistance if the methods students bring to the material are characterized as not particularly effective for the particular material at hand rather than summarily dismissing them in all situations.

A class may be presented with an example in which students can see for themselves that preexisting approaches clearly would not be effective in working with problems in the discipline. In several of my history courses, for example, I found that many students were resistant to explaining historical development in terms of social factors. As the work of Keith Barton and Linda Levstik (2002) has demonstrated, in the United States students at the primary and secondary levels tend to explain the past overwhelmingly in terms of the actions of individuals. This creates a very serious bottleneck at the college level, where it is impossible to understand contemporary historiography without the use of collective concepts such as class, gender, race, ethnicity, or national identity.

To deal with this particular obstacle to learning—as in most decoding—I needed to define precisely what experts in the field do that allows them to circumvent this potential bottleneck. Earlier interviews by the HLP had yielded several related mental operations that historians do automatically to deal with this tension between individual and collective perspectives. Most important, they are able to change perspective at will, sometimes viewing the world as an individual in the period under study would experience it and sometimes focusing on collective patterns. Students who are unable to make such a shift would be unable to successfully complete the work required in my course. Stuck in a world of individual actors and decisions, they are blocked from entering the world of contemporary historiography. But simply telling students that their individualistic models of human behavior are inadequate is as apt to produce emotional resistance and charges of ideological indoctrination as it is to produce real conceptual change. Therefore, I created a situation in which students themselves could see the limitations of the models that many of them brought to the course.

To develop a concrete metaphor to capture this process, I asked my students what they might say if they were asked by a friend what he or she could do to stop gaining weight. Unsurprisingly, the responses focused overwhelmingly on individual decisions, such as what to eat and how much to exercise. Then the students were told that across a great deal of the globe obesity rates were increasing at unprecedented rates; they were then asked to explain this phenomenon. They quickly realized that it was unreasonable to assume that hundreds of millions of people just happened to get up one morning and decide to eat more and exercise less, and they themselves began to seek societal factors that may have affected behavior on a larger scale.

In this process students on their own moved closer to a process of reasoning that was compatible with contemporary views of history. But it was stressed at the end of the process that if they were giving advice to a friend, it might still be useful to focus on individual decisions, although they could now realize that these decisions were not entirely independent of larger societal factors.

Thus, rather than my attempting to directly eradicate mental patterns that had worked for students in other situations, these students were themselves led to recognize the limitations of those ways of operating in the context of the course that they were taking. In this process of cognitive realignment, a potential for emotional resistance to learning had been neutralized before it could emerge.

Students can be involved in this process in other ways as well. If the initial assessment of student expectations about what they will be expected to do in the course has yielded a range of positions and includes some that approximate the methods actually used in the field, it can be very useful to present this gamut of possibilities and have the class discuss the possible virtues of each approach. This can become the basis for an exploration of why the strategies that are actually to be used in the course would work better for these particular intellectual problems than those expected by some of the students. At the end of the semester, students can be asked to write advice to a hypothetical friend or sibling on how to succeed in the course; their answers can often be presented to students in the next semester's class as an example of the approaches that actually work as opposed to those that the students may have assumed would be effective.

In efforts to defuse procedural bottlenecks, as in so much of decoding, it is important to disaggregate the mental operations involved. If, for example, students arrive in college convinced that the activity in many fields consists entirely of memorization, they are apt to be less willing to surrender this misconception if the alternatives seem to be an ill-defined mass of very demanding mental operations, all of which have to be mastered at once. If, however, these ways of

---

RESPONDING TO POTENTIAL PROCEDURAL EMOTIONAL BOTTLENECKS

Whatever the strategy used for modeling, the basic principles for dealing with procedural bottlenecks are the same:

1. As soon as possible, identify student ideas about how to succeed in the discipline.
2. Focus on those areas in which significant numbers of students misunderstand how the field works.
3. Begin modeling these operations before students naively begin playing by the wrong rules.
4. Create situations in which students themselves will see that their old approaches are not effective in the context of the course.
5. In many cases, leave open the possibility that their previous models might be appropriate in some other context.

operating are modeled clearly and sequentially, and if students are given a chance to practice each until they have mastered them, than the preconception about the nature of college work may dissolve quite naturally.

Identifying Narrative Bottlenecks

When we began Indiana University's Freshman Learning Project we were firmly focused on cognitive obstacles that interfered with student learning. As we proceeded, we increasingly recognized that issues of motivation also had to be considered, as well as students' incorrect assumptions about the kinds of work that were required in particular disciplines. But when the HLP began in-depth interviews with historians about the obstacles to learning in their courses, yet another sort of emotional bottleneck emerged. When asked to discuss places where students get stuck, some of our informants described situations in which learning was blocked by the resistance of students to the content of the course. One of our sources indicated that in a course on Latino history some of his students withdrew emotionally because they experienced negative information about the actions of Anglos in the past as criticisms of themselves and their families. Another indicated that her students were so emotionally involved with the notion that Native Americans should have been allowed to maintain their original culture that they were unwilling to engage with the growing literature indicating that these groups also actively worked to adjust to new living conditions.

But the problem was not limited to the history of minorities. Historians reported that in teaching about the American Revolution or U.S. participation in World War II, difficulties arose whenever the content of the course did not match the stories that the students had heard about these events as they were growing up.

We have every reason to believe that such negative emotional reactions to the content of college courses exist in a wide variety of disciplines. Students arrive in college with narratives about the world that will be held up for close scrutiny in many of the courses that they take. Even in the natural sciences, students sometimes have preconceived notions in their heads about such topics as evolution or climate change that can create obstacles to learning. They may perceive alternatives to their view of the subject matter as threatening to their well-being and may sense that the questioning that is encouraged in this environment could be a threat to their relationship with their families and with the community in which they were raised. In his celebrated article "On the Persistence of Unicorns," Craig Nelson notes that "learning critical thinking is existentially as well as intellectually challenging. In asking students to learn to think more critically, we ask them to set aside modes that have served them well and still tie them to family, friends, and prior teachers" (1999, 177–78). As Nelson has frequently observed in his presentations and workshops, what students learn in a college classroom may disrupt the once harmonious flow of opinions around the family dinner table. In some cases what they are studying may even be perceived as a betrayal of the family and the culture within which they have been raised.

As the proponents of threshold concepts have effectively pointed out, the liminal state between students' old worldview and the one presented by the disciplines they encounter in college can be very challenging. There may be a period in which the old points of view no longer have the same hold but new ones have not been entirely established. This uncertainty can be very distressing—particularly for students who have spent their previous lives in a world of absolute certainty.

As in the case of procedural emotional bottlenecks, it is important to get information early in the semester regarding student preconceptions about the subject matter of the course that might be in tension with material to be covered. Posing such questions can be a delicate matter, since students' answers might reinforce their preexisting opinions, or some might perceive the entire effort as a direct attack on their beliefs. Nonetheless, it is important to get some idea of where the members of a particular class stand on issues that could lead to emotional bottlenecks. Moreover, it can be useful early in the semester to get students to engage on an abstract level with some of the issues that might generate unproductive conflict later in the course.

Here, once again, the merger of decoding with Just-in-Time Teaching (JiTT) may yield productive possibilities. As was discussed in chapter 4, JiTT uses pre-class, online exercises to find out where students are having difficulties and to provide material for interactive sessions during class (Novak et al. 1999) In the context of emotional bottlenecks, this pattern could be used to get a clearer sense of beliefs that students bring to the course that are potentially in tension with material that will be encountered in the course. Many of the questions that Gregor Novak and Evelyn Patterson have already suggested for JiTT exercises in various disciplines could yield vital information about such preconceptions:

- *Introductory biology.* "What is the difference between a theory and a belief?"
- *Introductory earth science.* "When reading or hearing news reports of dinosaur discoveries, what questions should you think about and ask yourself to evaluate the accuracy of the reports?"
- *Economics.* "Imagine that you are a newspaper reporter assigned to write a story about the upcoming meeting of the Federal Open Market Committee. Make a list of three questions that you will want to ask. For each question, explain carefully why it is important and what answer you expect from the Committee." (Novak and Patterson 2010, 9)

To return to the examples from history provided above, one might imagine asking questions that would reveal a good deal about students' preconceptions and emotional investment in issues that are apt to come up in these courses:

- *Potential emotional bottleneck:* Many American students have idealized images of the founding fathers of the United States that make them resist more complex interpretations of the actions and interests of these political leaders.
  - *Question to reveal preconceptions:* To what extent, if any, is the fact that many of the signers of the Declaration of Independence were slaveholders relevant to our understanding of the American Revolution? Briefly explain the reasons for your answer.
- *Potential emotional bottleneck:* Many students idealize the life of Native Americans and hold so strongly to the image of these groups as passive victims that they are unable to consider the ways in which they acted to shape their roles in the broad society of the United States.
  - *Question to reveal preconceptions:* In what ways, if any, may the assimilation of poor peasant emigrants from southern Italy into mainstream U.S. culture be seen as similar to the "Americanization" of native peoples? In what ways is it different? Briefly explain your answer.
- *Potential emotional bottleneck:* Many students hold such an idealized vision of World War II as "the good war" that they reject any consideration of the complexities of American actions during the conflict as an unpatriotic attack on the nation and its heroes.
  - *Question to reveal preconceptions:* After World War II the United States and its allies conducted trials of German and Japanese citizens accused of committing atrocities during the conflict. War necessarily involves violence, but the trials were based in part on the belief that there were limits that must be respected even during wartime. Do such limits apply to a nation that is fighting a defensive war? Explain the reasons for your answer.

It is important to note that, in addition to providing useful information to the instructor, all of these questions have a potentially positive secondary effect: they also may create an occasion for at least some students to think more deeply about assumptions and attitudes that they bring to the course. For such students the nature of the question can problematize preexisting beliefs in a manner that does not involve the imposition of the instructor's position on them.

Minimizing the Negative Emotional Impact of Narrative Bottlenecks

Strategies such as these can provide invaluable information about the preconceptions that students bring to our courses, and these can help us become more aware of the potential for unproductive reactions to elements in the content we teach. But foreknowledge of emotionally explosive issues is not sufficient. We need strategies to prevent the emotions produced by these mismatches from overwhelming learning.

At this point it is important to stress once again that not all emotions are problematic in teaching. In dealing with dysfunctional emotions, the goal is not to remove all feelings or even all conflict from the classroom. Issues like race do involve strong emotions, and master teachers such as Peter Frederick (1995) have demonstrated that confronting powerful emotions in the classroom directly and explicitly can create some of the most powerful and transformative educational experiences that students will ever have. Students' strong feelings about certain topics we teach can give energy to a class, and a college course can be an ideal place to deal directly with crucial issues.

But to honor the occasions on which emotions can contribute to learning is not to deny that sometimes they can also bring it to a halt. The process can overheat, and students may attack or withdraw in a manner that shuts down learning. This problem is particularly serious in the kinds of conflicts over interpretation of subject matter that we are considering in this section. Here negative emotions often lead to angry attacks on the instructor or to a sullen withdrawal and a resolution by the student to go through the motions but to forget what has been "learned" as soon as the course is complete. Even worse, if they are translated into charges that the instructor is biased, the negative feelings of a student may manifest themselves in ways that interfere with the learning of other students. And strong preexisting beliefs that go unexamined can also contribute to unproductive interactions among students in which discussions degenerate into name-calling.

It is rarely effective to simply tell students that everything they have been told about a particular topic by their family, friends, and teachers is wrong. Instead we need strategies for engaging with the beliefs that students bring to our courses and for helping them to create bridges between what they have been told in the past and what is now being presented to them. We need to bring students to the point at which they themselves can make rational choices among competing explanations. And we need to remain aware that the experience of losing one's grasp on notions that have provided a sense of certainty in the world can lead to major trauma and to emotional crises.

Dealing with clashes between student narratives about course subject matter and the actual content of the course is a complex challenge, one that decoding has come to face relatively recently. We have no silver bullet to make these problems disappear, but our work to date suggests that some of the basic strategies used to respond to cognitive obstacles to learning may be relevant to emotional bottlenecks as well. Joan Middendorf's insight that emotional bottlenecks are parallel to the kinds of conflicts between preexisting concepts and disciplinary norms that have been studied in the natural sciences has opened up great possibilities. Using the strategies that have been developed by educational researchers such as Madeleine Chi, she has laid the foundations for the kind of direct engagement with this type of bottleneck that will be developed in the remainder of this chapter (Middendorf et al. 2015).

To deal with emotional bottlenecks arising from content it is useful to return to the three basic principles described in the first section of this chapter—to intervene before the potentially dysfunctional emotions fully emerge, to focus on the cognitive framework within which the problem is generated, and to look for mismatches between preconceptions and what students actually experience in the course. The application of the first and the third of these principles is relatively straightforward. If one finds year after year that learning is disrupted by a discrepancy between students' preexisting beliefs and some aspect of the content of the course, it is important to structure the course from day one to minimize the impact of this bottleneck. Once the dysfunctional emotions have been fully engaged, it will be difficult to prevent negative effects on learning. Thus, as with bottlenecks arising from student preconceptions about the nature of work in the disciplines, an instructor needs to gain information early about the range of beliefs that exists within the class, to anticipate how some of these might conflict with what is to be taught in the course, and to have strategies in place that minimize the negative impact of these preexisting beliefs.

The application of the second principle—the recognition of the interdependence of cognitive and affective factors—may seem at first to be counterintuitive. Given the fact that such problems generally manifest themselves in the form of open or covert emotional resistance to what is being taught, it may seem to be necessary to deal with the situation entirely on the emotional plane and, as has been noted above, this is often an appropriate response. But at the core of the decoding strategy is the conviction that feelings and intellectual concepts are integrally connected and reinforce one another. If embracing the notion that climate change is created by humans will create tension with people who are important to a student, there will be a natural tendency to avoid that conclusion. Conversely, having a set of cognitive patterns can predispose students to take certain positions and to invest emotional energy in them. Thus, students who do not understand the nature of scientific inquiry may thereby be predisposed to view the debates between mainstream climatologists and climate change deniers or between evolutionary biologists and their fundamentalist detractors as a shouting match between similar parties and then pick the side that most comfortably matches their preexisting preferences. (See, for example, Nelson 2012.) Thus, the cognitive manner in which a problem is approached can predispose an individual toward a particular emotional response, just as emotions can incline individuals toward particular forms of understanding (Cameron-Bandler and Lebeau 1986).

We have found that it is generally more effective to focus our attention on the cognitive aspects of this union of thought and feeling. Trying to change students' emotions directly often generates major resistance; giving them alternate ways to think about a problem is often much easier, and it can have greater long-term impact. But to achieve this kind of cognitive reorganization a certain distance from the topic is necessary. If students are already boiling inside because they perceive their instructor as trying to indoctrinate them in an alien ideology, they are not apt to carefully reconsider the manner in which they are approaching the issue at hand. Therefore, if students' cognitive approach contributes to the likelihood that dysfunctional emotions will appear, it will be a good idea to introduce them to different ways of processing material long before the potentially explosive material occurs in the course (Pace 2003).

The process of focusing on the cognitive framework within which emotional bottlenecks are generated does not need to involve any direct reference to the issues that are controversial for the students. If an instructor knows that the discussion of climate change that will come in week five of a course is apt to produce reactions from students that disrupt learning, it may be wise to initiate a serious consideration of what makes something credible in science in the first or second week—a discussion that does not need to involve climate change at all. Once the class has agreed on criteria for judging scientific claims in the abstract, the students will be in a much better position to consider the conflicting assertions of climatologists and their critics.

This process can be aided by decoding. As we have seen repeatedly, the cognitive framework within which potentially controversial issues are processed by experts in the field may be so automatic to them that elements within that framework are not conscious. This may have important implications in the affective as well as the cognitive realms. Experts in the discipline rarely experience the kinds of emotional resistance to the content of the field that prevents some students from learning. This resistance to the emotional bottleneck occurs, in part, because mental operations that are second nature to specialists create a very different experience of the subject matter. If those ways of operating that inoculate experts against these obstacles are successfully shared with students, the latter will be less likely to succumb to these difficulties. But to accomplish this end it is necessary to first have a clear sense of all these steps and to be sure that those that are most relevant to the emotional bottlenecks are identified, modeled, and assessed by the instructor and practiced by the students. Thus, explicitly teaching students how practitioners in the discipline approach the problem from the inside may help many of them to grapple more successfully with potentially disturbing issues.

Another way to establish this distance is to move the focus away from the interaction between the instructor and the student by letting students know that there is a range of opinions on the controversial issue within the class itself. Here Just-in-Time Teaching techniques can once again be useful. If questions such as those discussed above have been used to determine students' attitudes toward issues that might arouse opposition, the results of this survey might be made available anonymously to the class as a whole. A respectful discussion of the results could be conducted in class, during which the cognitive underpinnings of the different responses are considered. (For an excellent set of recommendations for using such responses in class, see Novak and Patterson 2010, 15.) This can yield a productive consideration of the assumptions and values that underlie some of the responses and a serious consideration of occasions on which particular ways of approaching issues are appropriate in specific situations (e.g., when questions of evidence or of faith may be most relevant). Whatever challenges to preexisting beliefs that arise in the discussion will be most likely perceived as coming from the position of other students, not imposed by the instructor. Moreover, the possibility that other members of the class might approach the issue from a very different direction might encourage students to think more seriously about their own ways of dealing with the issue. Finally, this approach applies the principle that it is best to intervene in the process before strong negative emotions have been evoked.

An Example of Decoding a Narrative Bottleneck

Thus far the discussion of dealing with the emotional bottlenecks generated by subject matter has been relatively abstract. Let us now consider a particular bottleneck that was described in one of the HLP interviews. One of our interviewees shared a problem that arose in the U.S. history survey when he discussed the movement in the mid-twentieth century of immigrants from abroad and of African Americans from the South into northern and western cities. He described the difficulties that all groups had in these transitions, but when he pointed out that African Americans faced particular problems that other groups were spared, there was a negative emotional response from some students. One student, for example, raised her hand and asked the instructor, "Are you saying that white immigrants had some role in the creation of segregation for African Americans—because my parents came to Louisville from Greece in the World War II period, and they had nothing to do with this." As others of our sources corroborated, such students often experience the material being studied in many history courses as undermining the moral legitimacy of their families and as an indirect attack on themselves. Once the issue has been framed in this way, the understandable emotional response is very apt to prevent these students from ever grasping the more subtle message of the instructor.

It is important at this point to pull back and think about the emotions that are at play here. It is not surprising that race would evoke strong emotions in a society that has been dealing with the residue of slavery for a century and a half; this is to be expected, and is a natural part of teaching this subject. But in this particular example, the emotions are evoked not just by the issue of race in itself but also from the perceived need of this student to protect her parents from moral condemnation. The defense of her family represented "noise" in the pedagogical system that was not likely to lead to any real learning. It was not the intention of the instructor to attack these two Greek immigrants in postwar Louisville; he was concerned with broader patterns of race, economics, and housing. It may be useful to engage directly with this student's feelings concerning race at some point, but the issue of the moral culpability of these two individuals is a red herring that interrupts the learning process.

It is thus worth focusing on this perception. On one level there was a simple conflict of narratives: the instructor recognized that the problem resulted in part from the mismatch between the stories such students brought to the course and the interpretations that contemporary historians have generated, and he indicated that the response of such students draws "on popular discourses that tell them that immigrants suffered, worked hard, and overcame, and so the notion that everyone who suffered did not have the same opportunities out of their suffering really troubles them."

But beneath this clash of narratives there was almost certainly a deeper cognitive mismatch. As will be discussed in chapter 8, more empirical research needs to be done in decoding cognitive frameworks that students bring to courses in particular disciplines. But based on the instructor's testimony, there is every reason to believe that the professor and the student were inhabiting conceptually different classrooms that day. For the professor this part of the course was about patterns of immigration and social and economic structures that produced very different options for immigrants from other countries and those from the rural south. The comments of the student suggest that her response rested upon the particular form of individualist folk anthropology that was discussed in an earlier example in this chapter. Within this worldview, history is entirely the result of individual decisions made more or less in isolation. From this point of view the new inhabitants of northern cities all made choices: those who made good choices should have prospered; those who made bad choices should have fallen behind. If black migrants to northern cities did not have the same opportunities, it must have been because white immigrants were somehow cheating. What seemed to be a generalization about historical patterns to the instructor became in the mind of his student a specific moral condemnation of the individual actions of her parents.

Presumably, if the student approached the issue in terms of the same intellectual categories as the instructor, this emotional confrontation would have been minimized. Within the framework of power structures and social attitudes inhabited by historians, very different feelings would be generated. Individuals are seen as acting in terms of a limited set of choices that are available to them. The options of different groups vary enormously, as do the possibilities available in different time periods; structural factors limit the opportunities of some groups more than others. As such, while particular individuals may have historically acted in ways that seem morally indefensible from our point of view today, they did so within a broader structure that was fundamentally unfair but that cannot be reduced to a simple calculus of good and bad individuals. From our perspective the entire system may be morally corrupt, and we may applaud those individuals who rose above the conditions of their era. But it does not make sense to explain the entire pattern of discrimination simply as the result of individuals making bad choices.

Within this intellectual context the goal of the historian is to reconstruct the horizon of possible actions of different groups in the past and to understand the intellectual and social factors that created such patterns. If students lack access to this way of conceptualizing the past, they will remain unable to understand what is being taught, and the possibilities of negative emotional responses will greatly increase. If they are introduced to this way of processing, there is much less likelihood of mismatches that derail learning. Within a world of shared cognitive structures the student and the professor might have very different emotional reactions to the significance of race in twentieth-century U.S. history, but they would not be fighting about whether two particular Greek immigrants were good people.

It is thus possible to imagine a response to this situation in which we evoke the three principles of decoding affective bottlenecks. The possibility of dysfunctional emotional responses at this point in the course would be lessened by reshaping students' perceptions of history beginning on the first day of class. There would be an attempt to diagnose both their understanding of how to think about individuals and groups in the past and their general narratives of U.S. history to become aware of any mismatches between what they are bringing to the class and what they will actually encounter that could create problems. There would be systematic efforts to model for students the kind of mental processes that historians use in analyzing phenomena such as racial inequity. The students would have opportunities to practice these ways of processing historical information in contexts that were less emotionally charged until they became automatic. And, finally, the instructor would assess the extent to which students were able to operate in terms of broader social structures before they were called upon to deal with issues that were highly charged.

It is important to recognize that this process would not, in itself, solve the problem of teaching race in the classroom. Race is obviously far too powerful a force in the world for all the dysfunctional emotional charge to be dissipated in a single course. A great deal more serious work in the scholarship of teaching and learning must be done before we have a better understanding of the kinds of emotional and cognitive patterns that make it so difficult for students—as for most of the rest of humankind—to deal with this explosive issue. And there is a good chance that the particular student whose response served as the trigger for this discussion might not be willing to face the intellectual and moral consequences of learning to process history in the manner that professional historians typically do, even if the path to those mental operations were made easier.

Hopefully, however, decoding can be a part of the effort to draw more students into a productive encounter with such emotionally charged subjects. If the course has been organized from the beginning around modeling the mental operations built into contemporary historiography, and the students have been given many chances to reconstruct the situations of different groups, it is likely that fewer students will emotionally disconnect from the course when potentially divisive material is presented. At the very least, decoding can help remove the smaller obstacles to dealing with such issues—like the confusion of a description of broad historical patterns with the moral status of two Greek immigrants. And it is quite possible that such systematic exploration of the obstacles to learning in this area can begin to chip away at the giant emotional bottleneck of race in the classroom.

The details of this example are, of course, specifically relevant to history and related disciplines. But the pattern of response can be the same in any field: identify places where negative emotions are hindering the learning of some students, define the discrepancy between the way that professionals in the field process the material and what students bring to the course, and act early and often to provide students with mental operations that are more functional in this situation.

The emphasis in all this work is upon giving students the tools they need to view the phenomena being studied from new perspectives. The choice of whether to accept the interpretations that have come to dominate the discipline remains theirs. This is, of course, in part the acceptance of an inevitability: we simply do not have the power to force students to feel in particular ways, and blatant efforts to impose particular perspectives on them often have the effect of strengthening preexisting beliefs. But many of our students do not have a choice when they arrive in our classrooms. They are locked into narrow ways of processing information that limit their possibilities, and they react automatically without considering other ways of viewing issues. Providing them a choice among alternate ways of understanding the world can be a gift of freedom that goes far beyond anything else that we have to teach in the course.

((6.)) ASSESSMENT

By now it is—or should be—something of a cliché to stress that gaining meaningful evidence about student learning is a prerequisite of good teaching. We are hopefully past the days in which instructors were satisfied that they could assess the success of a course through their interpretation of visual clues from the students in the first row of an auditorium. There is increasing awareness that, unless there is reliable information flowing back to the instructor about the extent to which students are mastering the targeted mental operations, the efforts of a teacher are as aimless as those of an army without an intelligence unit. With no clear sense of the problems that need to be addressed and the success that one is having at addressing them, an instructor is left flying blind.

Academics have, of course, been testing their students at least since the beginning of the university system. But the focus has generally been on ranking students rather than on exploring the learning process and determining what changes might make it more effective. Operating within this traditional framework, instructors have generally focused on summative evaluations that determine whether students have or have not mastered material and skills from the course as a whole. Such forms of assessment have two disadvantages. In the first place they often come too late to help the students in a particular course. As Gregor Novak (2010) has argued, the traditional final exam is an autopsy; it might possibly provide some information to the instructor, but it is too late to help the student.

The second limitation of traditional forms of testing is even more serious. They tend to measure large, complex conglomerations of skills and thus provide little information about precisely what is missing in the student's conceptual tool kit. To extend Novak's metaphor, it is as if the autopsy only provided the information that an individual was dead without offering an understanding of why the death occurred. Traditional, summative exams tend to be global, requiring students to simultaneously employ multiple mental operations. Thus, while success is an indication that a student has some control over an entire set of skills, failure generally provides little or no useful information about which abilities are still missing. What is needed are forms of assessment that provide specific

Traditional Testing	Decoding Assessment
• Seeks to sort successful students from those who are not successful	• Seeks to identify which operations students have mastered
• Poses global challenges that require the mastery of multiple skills	• Poses focused challenges that require mastery of specific skills
• Provides over-all information about whether student has succeeded or not	• Provides specific feedback about which skills a student has mastered

information about the areas in which students have or have not mastered the particular mental operations required in the discipline at hand. Such feedback should be available to students and instructors throughout the course, and it should provide explicit information about the extent to which students are mastering specific operations.

All of this is not to deny that traditional testing still has a role in many situations. There is often a need to determine whether students have mastered an entire process or to certify that they are qualified to pass to the next level or to function as professionals in the field. But the decoding process requires different forms of inquiry.

The Decoding the Disciplines process depends upon a free flow of information at every stage of teaching. As we have seen repeatedly, at the beginning of a course it is important to know not only the basic places where students typically get struck but also the preconceptions that students typically bring to a course. Throughout the semester it is important to make course corrections and to help students who are still having difficulty. Moreover, decoding is intended to be an iterative process, and there is no expectation that all efforts to overcome particular bottlenecks will necessarily be successful the first time that they are attempted. Therefore, it is vital to gather information about which interventions are working and which will need to be reevaluated before the course is taught again. And finally, since the sharing of one's experience with others is an essential part of the process (as we shall see in chapter 7), it is also important to have evidence of what happened in a course to offer to others. None of this is possible if one does not have a reliable base of information.

Therefore, assessment is an essential element in decoding. However, it is important to recognize that for the instructor, as for the military commander, the information coming in is almost always ambiguous and incomplete. This ambiguity is captured effectively in a passage by Lee Shuman that is worth quoting at length:

> At the very core of any field that we call a profession is an inherent and inescapable uncertainty. Professions deal with those parts of the world that are characterized by unpredictability. Teachers can teach in the same manner to three classes in a row and experience different consequences each time. Professions (like teaching) deal with that part of the universe where design and chance collide. One cannot resolve that uncertainty by writing new rules. The way forward is to make that collision, that unpredictability in our fields, itself an object of individual and collective investigation. We will never fully remove the uncertainty from teaching any more than we can from such other professions as clinical medicine, architecture, economic planning, or clinical social work. But as a profession, we can grow much wiser about how to anticipate and deal with uncertainty. (1999, 15)

This can be disturbing since, like many of our students, we would like to have hard, cold facts that we can build upon with certainty. Frustration with ambiguous information often leads instructors to fantasies of double-blind experiments in which all extraneous variables are stripped away and a clear and indisputable truth emerges about the nature of our students' learning and the success of our interventions. But—as Shulman indicates—in practice, the conditions for creating such unchallengeable evidence are almost never present. There are almost always extraneous factors that cannot be stripped away, and this makes it impossible to isolate a specific teaching strategy from all the other things that affect student learning. No two groups of students are ever exactly the same, and a variable as seemingly random as the time of day that a class is offered can have a great impact on the learning that occurs. Moreover, teaching almost always involves a personal relationship of some kind, and the personalities of the participants inevitably have an impact on learning. When it is possible to find data from hundreds of courses, we can often arrive at statistically meaningful conclusions. (See, for example, Hake 1998.) But within the sample size that is available to the great majority of instructors, it is almost never possible to compare two teaching situations that are identical except for a single variable.

Assessments of student learning will, therefore, rarely have the precision or replicability of many measurements in the natural sciences. This should not, however, prevent us from trying to develop reasonable criteria for evaluating student skills or the effectiveness of various teaching interventions. In this respect teaching and learning are like 99 percent of human experience. In almost every aspect of our lives we are faced with situations in which we are unable to operate with absolute certainty but are able to develop processes that narrow down the possibilities and thus determine that certain courses of action are more promising than others. The fuzziness of consumer choices does not drive advertisers to abandon all attempts to understand what sells, and the difficulty in evaluating precisely what makes a great athletic performance has not prevented sports medicine from devising effective means of improving the functioning of athletes. The goal of the scholarship of teaching and learning can only be the development of the firmest assessment processes available for the situations within which we teach.

It is at this point that the decoding process becomes particularly useful to assessment. The identification of common bottlenecks (step 1) can suggest which skills need to be most carefully observed across the course. Once the necessary operations have been defined and broken up into their constituent parts (step 2), instructors can begin the process of creating occasions for evaluating how well students have learned each of these specific processes. Through decoding, assessment can become purpose driven and focused, and it can provide truly useful feedback that allows both students and instructors to work more effectively.

Given the misuse that has occurred in the realm of assessment, it is worth stressing that all of the assessments discussed in this chapter and on the Decoding the Disciplines website (http://decodingthedisciplines.org/step-6-assessing -student-learning/) have been based on the goals and practices of professionals in the disciplines themselves. They are all focused on giving instructors clearer information about what their students are learning so that they can adjust their classroom activities to help students do better at assimilating the ways of thinking that have been developed within the field of study. Even the larger-scale assessments described are to be viewed as an indigenous, departmental response to shared conceptions of teaching rather than something imposed from outside the discipline. They are to be seen as a means of increasing learning, not distinguishing "good" and "bad" teachers or departments. Anything else would create a disjunction between what is being measured and what is really going on in courses.

The Qualities of a Decoded Assessment

The central strategy of decoding assessment is to get very specific about what we want students to do. The essential words in this formulation are *specific* and *do*. Vague questions about generic "critical thinking" will only result in vague results that are of very limited use in creating real increases in student learning in particular courses.

Specificity also allows us to separate degrees of student mastery. By breaking up complex tasks into discrete operations, we are able to provide students with useful information about what skills they have or have not mastered, what progress they have made in each area, and what is the next appropriate step in their learning. This also offers the instructor more precise information about which areas need more work and which are succeeding as they stand.

The second element in decoding assessment is emphasis on what students need to *do* rather than what they need to *know*. In any field, of course, a certain level of background knowledge is needed, and sometimes it is important to evaluate what information students have about the material at hand. But learning problems are much more likely to be produced by students' inability to master basic disciplinary operations than by the absence of particular facts in their minds.

Therefore, assessments must create situations in which students' ability to do specific tasks can be observed. At the core of the process are two questions:

1. What would it look like if a student did this operation correctly?
2. What do student mistakes tell us about what is missing in the learning process?

Assessments at the Beginning of a Course

Every course rests upon certain assumptions about the disciplinary skills of the students, their factual knowledge about the topic, their understanding of what is required for success in the discipline, and their general attitudes toward the issues that will be discussed. If these assumptions are incorrect, the instructor can be blindsided so seriously that it may be impossible to ever establish a productive learning environment. Patterns of bottlenecks that are typical for students in a discipline may not actually correspond to those present in a particular class. The students may need to have certain mental operations modeled for them that were not part of the original plan for the course. Conversely, if one does not have clear information about the particular set of students that one is teaching, time may be wasted on skills that the students have already mastered. There may be significant differences in the skills and sophistication of different portions of the class that need to be taken into consideration. And, as we have seen in chapter 5, student preconceptions about the nature of the discipline or the subject matter to be covered may create emotional land mines that can blow up in the face of an instructor who is not aware of these possibilities.

Therefore, it is generally very useful to gain some information about the particular spectrum of students at the beginning of a course. (Here, once again, I must emphasize the debt I owe to my History Learning Project colleagues at Indiana University, Leah Shopkow and Arlene Díaz, for much of what follows.) To get a sense of students' understanding of the discipline and of the kinds of work needed to succeed in it, one might ask students to answer a question such as "Doing work in history is most like . . ." or "Preparing for an exam in psychology is most like . . ." and then provide several possibilities among which to choose. If it is likely that students have already taken a course in the discipline, an instructor might ask them what they found most difficult in the field or what they liked most or least about it. Or one can ask for a one-paragraph summary of the field. Such initial assessments can provide useful information about the preconceptions about the discipline that students bring to a course at a moment when it is still possible to make course corrections that will more clearly model the kinds of work that will really be expected of the students.

If there are specific kinds of activities that are crucial to the course, such as work in collaborative teams or in the lab, it can be very helpful to know in advance what expectations about such activities students bring to the class. Asking students to briefly describe their previous experiences in such situations can help instructors know when the purposes of crucial class procedures need to be explained more fully and where certain ways of operating need to be modeled. Such questions may also allow the instructor to create collaborative learning teams in which those students who are enthusiastic about group work can affect the behavior of their team mates.

If instructors have experienced particular bottlenecks in previous versions of their courses, or if decoding work has identified common obstacles to learning in the discipline, it can be very useful to note the extent to which these may be present in a particular class. If, for example, the task of isolating the crucial concept in a passage is a common obstacle to learning in the study of history, the instructor could give students a paragraph and ask them to identify the most important idea. In a geology class it might be useful to give a small task to students to see if they are able to deal effectively with switching time frames. If in a literature class the instructor suspects the students might have trouble understanding the nature of literary analysis, he or she might give students a passage and ask them to list the questions they might ask themselves if they were writing a paper on the topic.

As we have seen in chapter 5, it can be very helpful to have a sense of what emotional bottlenecks may be lying in wait to interrupt learning. These can be difficult to identify, and there may be some danger of intensifying certain dysfunctional attitudes by bringing them to the surface. But these problems can generally be avoided either by asking questions obliquely or by concentrating on the cognitive patterns that sustain potentially destructive preconceptions. Taking the first strategy, an instructor in a biology class might ask students not what they themselves believe about evolution but what they have heard about the topic. Or the same instructor might choose to explore the cognitive framework within which students approach the issue by asking students how they would define such terms as *scientific theory, hypothesis,* or *proof.* Such questions can provide an initial idea of the worldview that particular students may have prior to taking this particular course, and thus show the instructor whether it is necessary to create modeling experiences that will expand students' notions about the field.

Using the Practice as a Means of Assessment

Once a course has begun, assessments can often flow seamlessly from practice and feedback, step 4 in the decoding process. If they are studied systematically, the results of such assignments and exercises can provide useful information about the level of student mastery of basic skills at crucial moments in the course.

As has been noted in chapter 1, students are very generous in providing us with evidence of their inability to perform the basic tasks required in our disciplines, but we often do not devote sufficient attention to taking advantage of their largess.

In chapter 4 we saw how chemistry professor Jill Robinson found that her students were facing a bottleneck because they tried to memorize the solutions to problems and plug them into new situations without pausing to consider what was really called for. She modeled the processes by which chemists analyze what is needed to solve a problem and, in order to give her students practice, she gave them multistep problems and asked them not to answer the questions but to instead list the steps they would take to find a solution. To determine whether her efforts had been successful, she compared the students' plans for solving problems from the beginning of the modeling/practice process with those at the end and found that the scores had increased from 30 percent to 70 percent. If she had simply asked the students to solve the problems, the resulting data would not have given her clear information about the change in her student's understanding of the process of problem solving in the discipline because success or failure would have been the result of a variety of different factors. By narrowing the process down to a focus on the steps involved in problem solving, Robertson obtained more precise information about what skills students had mastered.

Just-in-Time Teaching techniques can be combined with decoding to produce positive results in this area, as in so many others. Warm-up exercises that require mastery of the same mental operation can be assigned at the beginning and the end of a course, and a comparison of the results can provide an indication of the extent of student progress. Thus, the same exercise that served to reinforce modeling and to provide students with an opportunity to practice and receive feedback can also serve as a form of assessment.

The nature of such assessments will, of course, vary greatly from discipline to discipline, but to provide a clearer picture of the seamless transition from step 4 (practice and feedback) to step 6 (assessment), here are some examples from my own courses. In this class on culture and society in Paris in the second half of the nineteenth century I gave students an assignment that required them to imagine that they were writing a paper on male and female gender roles during that period. I did not ask them to actually write the paper, because that would involve too many complex tasks; instead, since I was particularly concerned at this point in the course with helping students develop and defend historical interpretations, I asked them to (1) present a thesis for the hypothetical essay; (2) state three propositions that they would need to defend to make that interpretation credible; (3) present a piece of evidence that could be used to support each proposition; and (4) explain how that evidence supported the appropriate proposition.

The process of isolating each of these four operations within the structure of the assignment allowed me to see which skills particular students had mastered and where they needed more support. To organize this process I created a rubric for each operation, assigned a point or some fraction thereof to each part of a student's assignment, and entered the results on a spreadsheet. The results of this tabulation were reassuring: five of the thirteen students got a perfect score, receiving full credit for their examples of propositions, supporting evidence, and justifications for the choices of evidence. As a group, the class averaged a score of 93 out of a possible 100 on the final iteration.

It can also be useful to follow the trajectory of individual students through a series of exercises, focused on a common operation or closely connected operations. In another of my courses I picked a student who had mastered many of the basic skills needed in an upper-level history course but who had not moved from the B+ to the A level. I focused on three areas of weakness in the paper produced in the first week: explaining the relevance of evidence in supporting an interpretation, generating historical theses, and producing analyses that probed beneath the surface. I identified parts of the weekly online assignments that targeted each of these operations and compared the student's performance on these tasks across the semester. I also analyzed his success at employing each of these operations in two long papers written near the end of the semester. It was clear that there was steady improvement in each of these areas across the semester, suggesting that, at least in this case, the in-class modeling and online exercises were at least moving the student in the right direction, even if he had not made the full transition in a single semester.

The precise nature of the assessments will, of course, depend on the nature of the discipline, but if an instructor has created forms of practice that focus very specifically on individual mental operations, it is generally quite easy to get a clear idea of the extent to which students are mastering them. The crucial step here, as in the decoding process generally, is to reduce vague forms of critical thinking to specific operations and to focus practice on each of these. Once this has been done, assessment becomes almost trivial.

Special Activities that Provide Information on Student Mastery

In addition to assessments that flow directly from decoded assignments, it is often useful to create special activities that generate additional information about students' mastery of essential mental operations. The kinds of classroom assessment techniques developed by Thomas Angelo and K. Patricia Cross (1993) can be very useful in this quest for ways to make student learning visible. Such simple diagnostic tools as Minute Papers, Word Journal, Concept Maps, or just asking students to write the most important idea that emerged from a class can provide a window into the ways in which students are operating in the discipline. These tools have the advantage of being simple and brief, and they can provide very regular information about student functioning in the course that allows timely readjustments of teaching strategies.

Sometimes the assessment process is indirect, as when I ask my students at the end of a course to write a letter to a hypothetical friend or sibling who will be taking the class in the future and to describe what they should do to succeed. I have indications that certain of my goals for the students have been at least partially successful when I encounter responses such as: "First, what a history class in college is not. It is not a math class. There are no clear formulas that produce exacting answers. There is no one correct interpretation, or even two or three necessarily. Interpreting an event in history means compiling evidence and making some decisions." Another student wrote, "Be able to immerse yourself in the world—the place and the period. Adopt the mind-set of the people you are studying." In these case there is evidence that students have managed to get past obstacles that often thwart learning in history classes (e.g., not adapting to the particular ways of operating in the discipline, assuming that history is a matter of piling up facts, rather than advancing possible interpretations, or failing to understand that it is crucial to re-create the worldview and experience of individuals and groups from past eras).

My History Learning Project colleagues Arlene Díaz and Leah Shopkow have demonstrated considerable creativity in creating visual assignments that reveal student mastery of essential operations or the lack thereof (Shopkow et al. 2013a). They have asked students to turn elements from literary texts (*Beowulf, El Cid,* descriptions of events by Aztec and European observers) into images and have then used the presence or absence of crucial elements as an indicator of the depth of student understanding of the material. For example, the presence of much blood in student representations of the Aztecs, but its absence in their drawings of the equally violent texts about the medieval Spanish hero El Cid, provided useful information about the ways in which the cultural preconceptions of Díaz's students were shaping their ability to place developments in a historical context. And both Leah and Arlene have developed strategies for replacing traditional final exams with sessions in which learning teams present carefully articulated interpretations of key material via poster sessions. These tasks are precisely framed in ways that make the presence or absence of key mental operations apparent (Shopkow et al. 2013a).

Pre- and Posttests

Most of the assessments that we have considered give a snapshot of student learning at particular moments in a course. But sometimes we may need to produce special exercises that make changes in student learning even more visible, frequently in the form of pre- and posttests that focus on a single operation or set of operations. These are particularly useful if one is planning to share what has been done in a formal presentation or publication in the scholarship of teaching and learning (see chapter 7).

For the purposes of decoding, such assessments should produce information about students' mastery of specific skills rather than their knowledge of the particular content of the course. Thus, it is important to create situations in which it is obvious whether or not students are employing a specific mental operation. A particularly effective example of this kind of assessment can be found in the Beyond the Bubble website produced by Sam Wineburg and his colleagues at Stanford University.[1] In an effort to isolate high school students' ability to conduct a crucial operation in history—clearly relating sources to the period in which they were created—Wineburg and colleagues presented a painting of the first Thanksgiving, with the name of the artist and the date of its creation (1932). Students were then asked to describe very briefly whether the image might be used to help us understand what actually happened on this occasion. In the answers it was easy to determine whether students recognized that a work produced in the first half of the twentieth century was of limited use in understanding an event that took place more than three centuries earlier, and this was a clear indicator of the extent to which they had mastered a key skill in history, regardless of their background knowledge of the period.

Such questions can be posed to students at the beginning and the end of a course, the answers can be coded and randomized by a third party, and then each response can be scored by one or more experts in the field. When the answers are sorted into pre- and posttest groups, it should be clear whether there has been in increase in student mastery across the semester. In courses in which the number of students make the reading of all answers too time-consuming, it is possible to evaluate a random sample of each group or to replace open-ended questions with multiple choice ones. It can be useful to test the assessment in advance with small groups of students to be sure that the instructions are clear and that the instructor's wording carries the intended connotations. And it may require several iterations before the pre- and posttests successfully capture the learning of a class.

Interviews with students conducted near the end of the semester provide another way to assess student learning. Ideally, the interviews would be videotaped by third parties, and the students would know that their responses will not be made available to the instructor until after the course grades have been submitted. But even if this is not practical, a simple conversation with students at the end of the semester can provide invaluable information about how they are responding to modeling and practice in the course. It is generally better to begin with very general questions (e.g., "Were there ways in which this course was different from most of the other courses that you have taken in similar fields?") and proceed to more detailed ones that focus on the specific operations that were explicitly taught in the course (e.g., "If you take another course in this area, what have you learned about geological time that will be important to remember?").

Assessing Decoding Itself

There remains the issue of assessing the effectiveness of decoding itself as a methodology. Throughout the present volume, strong claims have been made concerning the power of this tool for increasing learning, and the anecdotal observations of individual instructors using this approach have been very encouraging. Many instructors using assessments such as those described above have noted levels of learning and of student engagement in their courses that seemed much higher than in earlier iterations of the same courses. But are there any more solid reasons for believing that decoding can actually produce the results that are claimed for it?

This is a very demanding question. As has been suggested earlier in this chapter, the assessment step of the decoding process produces evidence concerning student mastery of specific mental operations in particular courses. Pre- and posttests, and interviews with students after they have taken decoded classes, have strongly suggested that student mastery of key mental operations was increased. But given the sample size and the absence of data from nondecoded courses, it is impossible to say with total assurance that it was decoding that made the difference.

To a certain extent an exhaustive analysis of the impact of decoding will need to wait until it is used with much larger numbers of students. But our one initial foray into this type of study, as part of the work of the History Learning Project, has yielded positive results. Around six hundred students from eight history courses were given a series of questions designed to test their ability to think historically. Presented with a set of historical sources concerning the Spanish-American War, they were asked four questions concerning how they might make use of these documents in a hypothetical paper and given several possible answers for each. The choices offered to the students were ranked by professional historians from five (most closely resembling historians' ways of operating) to one (most distant from professional historians' responses).

When the results were tabulated, the mastery of some of the key mental operations involved in studying history in the three courses that had been redesigned using decoding could be compared with those in the five courses developed in a more conventional manner. The students from the decoded classes did better on all four questions. These results were statistically significant, and a survey of the demographics of the classes yielded no other factor that seemed to account for the difference. Moreover, the students from the decoded courses did better even on mental operations that had not been explicitly modeled in their class, suggesting that once students began operating more effectively within the mental universe of the discipline they were able to generalize these ways of thinking to other areas (Shopkow et al. 2013a). It is to be hoped that as decoding becomes more common, studies of this sort will proliferate.

Modeling through Assessment

Decoding reminds us of the magnitude of the task we face as educators at the same time that it provides us with means to achieve that job more effectively. If we are to conscientiously meet our responsibility to students, we must do far more than reread the proverbial yellowing notes at the front of a lecture hall. We must identify the places where the learning of many students is blocked, make explicit the mental operations that they must master to get past these obstacles, and then model, give practice, and assess these processes. And yet, the time that we have to spend with our students remains the same. Technology may help us expand the opportunities to affect our students' learning a bit, but we still have to think seriously about how we can use the time that we do have in the most efficient manner possible.

One way to accomplish this is to try whenever possible to achieve several goals with the same action. Just as practice can serve as an occasion to support modeling (see chapters 3 and 4), assessment (step 6) can reinforce both modeling (step 3) and practice (step 4). While it is important to keep these three steps of the decoding process conceptually distinct, assessment should not be seen entirely as a process that exists apart from these other aspects of teaching and learning. Whenever practical, assessments should be viewed not only as a means of determining what students have learned but also of contributing to that learning itself. The structure of the task itself can reinforce these mental patterns and to give students yet another opportunity to practice them.

This aspect of teaching has been captured nicely by John Bransford, Ann Brown, and Rodney Cocking in a passage on successful assessments that is worth quoting in full:

> An important feature of assessments in these classrooms is that they be learner-friendly: they are not the Friday quiz for which information is memorized the night before, and for which the student is given a grade that ranks him or her with respect to classmates. Rather, these assessments should provide students with opportunities to revise and improve their thinking (Vye et al. 1998), help students see their own progress over the course of weeks or months, and help teachers identify problems that need to be remedied (problems that may not be visible without the assessments). (2000, 83)

Taking full advantage of this opportunity to combine assessment with modeling and practice requires conscious attention, however. Questions about procedures for solving problems can be mixed with those that directly ask students to employ these ways of operating. To return to the example of accounting used in chapter 2, if a bottleneck in the field is students' assumption that their job is to apply one model to all tax problems, then an instructor might present them with a particular problem and ask them to examine two different ways of approaching it. This would provide information about whether the students can actually generate more than one plausible response to the question at the same time that it reinforces their understanding that the consideration of multiple perspectives is a necessary part of working in the field.

The wording of assessments can be tweaked so that students are reminded of basic disciplinary patterns. The instructions, for example, may be couched in terms of a hypothetical situation in which a particular issue might arise (e.g., "Imagine that you were defending this interpretation in a paper . . ." or, "Imagine you were conducting an experiment on ＿＿ and encountered these data . . ."). This can serve to connect the specific tasks being required with the larger question of operating in the discipline. Or the question to be answered may be preceded with explicit reminders of some of the mental patterns that are needed in the field. To return to some of the common bottlenecks discussed in chapter 1, the fact that law students commonly focus on the sensational details of a case and ignore the basic legal principles embedded in it might lead an instructor to begin a question with an introductory clause such as "Since lawyers have to always identify the underlying legal principles beneath the surface details, how would you . . . ?" A historian of music might ask, "Since one of the major challenges facing someone studying music is to identify those features that distinguish one musical style or genre from another, what would you look for in Baroque music that would indicate its style?"

This combination of modeling, practice, and assessment can also be used as a tool for helping students think metacognitively about their own learning beyond the mastery of particular mental operations. As in the example above, tasks can be structured to encourage students to think more seriously about the process of doing something like writing a paper. As Gregor Novak and his colleagues have demonstrated, such knowledge about learning itself can be increased after an assignment or classroom assessment technique has been completed by showing the entire class the range of responses and discussing what makes some better than others or what might have led some students to follow a less effective path (Novak et al. 1999).

The details and the form of such assessment/assignments would, of course, vary greatly with the discipline, the size of the class, and the skills level of the students. But the basic principle of using assessments to reinforce modeling applies quite generally. A single course provides relatively limited occasions for creating deep and lasting changes in student learning, and we need to make choices that simultaneously contribute to multiple goals.

Assessment and the Metacognition of Instructors

One of the most important functions of decoding assessments is their effect on the metacognition of instructors themselves. When assessments are functioning appropriately, they provide regular information not only about what is happening in students' minds but also the extent to which the ideas that we have about teaching our field correspond to reality. Do we understand what is really required for success in our discipline? Are there crucial steps in the process that we have omitted? Do the metaphors and other means we use to model basic operations have meaning for our students? Are the opportunities that we provide for practicing these skills sufficiently focused and repeated to help those students with weaker skills to internalize the skills essential for success in the course? Do some students have preexisting conceptions or emotional orientations that we have not recognized and that are interfering with the learning process? And, perhaps most important, who are we really teaching and who are we only *pretending* to teach?

To use language from another era, at its best decoding can serve as a form of dialectical praxis in which we act on the world, receive back information about the inadequacies of our intellectual representations, and then act again with an altered model, slowly developing ever more accurate understanding of what is required to increase student learning. But this only works if we are constantly and systematically taking in targeted information about what is happening in our classes and altering the process of our teaching to match our new comprehension of the effect of our actions.

This is, of course, an intellectually demanding and time-consuming process. As such, the full realization of the potential of decoding will exceed the resources available to many—perhaps most—individual instructors. But the good news is that it is not necessary to do all the work on one's own. If the existence of the History Learning Project demonstrates anything, it is that it is no longer necessary to carry all the burdens of developing new ways to foster student learning by oneself. As we will see in chapter 7, decoding can contribute to opening a new era of shared experience in which what each instructor learns in his or her classroom can be more readily shared with colleagues around the world through a community of teacher-scholars.

7. SHARING

A GENERATION AGO, a pedagogical silence smothered innovation in teaching. What happened in the classroom stayed in the classroom. Instructors had to solve the problems that arose in that space on their own, even though colleagues down the hall faced the same challenges. In teaching there was no equivalent to the rich network of scholars who built on each other's work in the realm of traditional disciplinary research. This "pedagogical solitude," to use Lee Shuman's apt phrase, made teaching a lonely vocation, since the students rarely, if ever, fully understood the moves that their instructors were making in the classroom, and teachers were generally left with no one who could share in the victories and setbacks (Shulman 1993). And it also meant that brilliant solutions to common problems disappeared when their creators went into retirement (Bernstein 2002).

The Decoding the Disciplines process came into being in a very different social world. From the very beginning it has always been a profoundly collaborative undertaking, emerging from a collective effort to increase student learning. At every stage a variety of individuals has contributed essential insights, experiences, and energy to its development. And, as decoding has taken shape, it has become a very effective tool for developing a shared language about teaching and learning and for undertaking collective tasks.

Thus, it is not surprising that step 7 of the decoding process is sharing. In part this emerges from a sense of ethical responsibility. At the very core of decoding—and more broadly of the scholarship of teaching and learning (SoTL) in general—is the notion that knowledge about ways to increase student learning is best generated collaboratively and shared freely. This collaborative quality is captured in the various terms that have been used to capture the space within which SoTL occurs: "community property" (Shulman 1993), the "teaching commons" (Huber and Hutchings 2005), or the "trading zone" (Mills and Huber 2005). Within such a social landscape none of us can claim full credit for the pedagogical innovations we create because they are always built upon foundations laid by others, and this imposes an obligation to share what we have produced with a larger community.

Sharing also has a self-interested element. Decoding requires effort and creativity that deserve recognition. Having an audience of peers helps reenergize teaching and can establish a psychological and social feedback process that keeps pedagogical innovation going. But it also serves a more institutional function of legitimizing and potentially rewarding the labor put into improving instruction. So long as teaching is treated as an entirely private matter, there is little chance that it will ever find a real place in the reward system of most institutions of higher education. The act of presenting what one has learned about teaching and learning, formally or informally, is a necessary precondition for the incorporation of this aspect of our professional lives within processes of reward and recognition.

But beyond its ethical, psychological, and institutional advantages, there is a very practical reason for making sharing an integral part of the decoding process. Sharing is not just an extraneous element added onto a process of exploration—the equivalent of the nineteenth-century explorer bringing specimens back to display in the gentlemen's clubroom. Instead, the process of making one's investigations visible to others is actually a part of the exploration itself. As Pat Hutchings and Mary Huber note, "the scholarship of teaching and learning is not really finished until it is captured in ways that others can see and examine. . . . Going public is not simply a final step in the process—a *t* to be crossed or an *i* to be dotted; instead, it creates new lenses and angles on the entire process and the significance of the work" (Huber and Hutchings 2005, 27).

An occasion for externalizing what one is trying to do in the classroom thus very frequently leads to new insights in SoTL, just as the process of sharing traditional disciplinary research expands one's understanding. The old saw so often repeated to students—that one does not fully understand something until it has been explained to someone else—seems to apply equally well to instructors.

But such sharing does not have to wait until a project is completed. It can occur at any stage in the process. For simplicity of presentation we have made sharing the seventh step in the decoding process, but this should not be interpreted in a narrowly chronological sense. It is certainly not necessary to wait until one has passed through all the earlier steps to begin working with others. It can begin at any stage of this work.

Fortunately, decoding itself can make such collaboration easier. Those who are immersed in the process have at their disposal a shared language for defining both the difficulties posed by their discipline and potential responses to these challenges. The focus on bottlenecks and the exploration of disciplinary operations, as well as the other steps of decoding, provide a framework that makes it easier for one instructor to build on the work of another. This allows the accumulation of knowledge about what works in a particular discipline, and that can produce real changes.

The sharing process also facilitates the application of new insights into teaching far beyond the individual course in which they were first generated. As we shall see later in this chapter, the decoding paradigm can provide a central, organizing framework within which to address the problems in a department, a campus, or an entire discipline. By providing a point of focus and a shared language for talking about problems, it has the potential of uniting energies at all levels of academia.

But taking full advantage of these opportunities requires the creation of communities of practice in which the challenges of teaching can be faced collectively and the fruits of decoding can be freely and safely shared. At the simplest level, sharing may take the form of informal conversations with colleagues. At the next level, the decoding process may be shared through formal or informal faculty learning communities. The next levels involve sharing within departments, then institutions, and finally within entire disciplines. At the broadest level sharing can take the form of SoTL papers and publications that allow the entire community of scholarly teachers to see the results of an individual or a team's experiments in decoding. But at all levels the practice can be greatly enriched through sharing.

Communities of Decoding Practice

Decoding the Disciplines emerged within a community of practice—Indiana University's Freshman Learning Project (FLP)—and such small groups of committed faculty can provide a particularly effective framework for making this paradigm a living part of the teaching practice in an institution. This environment can be replicated either in formally constituted programs, such as the FLP, or in informal groups that meet regularly to share efforts to define and overcome bottlenecks.

In the early years of the FLP we experimented briefly with bringing together instructors from closely related fields, but we found that there was a special power in interactions among instructors from very different disciplines. One of the main functions of decoding is to make teachers more aware of the particular nature of their discipline and to understand that the ways of operating that are automatic to them may seem very foreign to their students. An intense encounter with instructors from other fields can help us escape from the disciplinary silos in which we are apt to be trapped.

In the FLP we intensified this experience through a number of intentional strategies. As an icebreaker we asked groups of instructors in similar fields to generate statements that would be intelligible to those in a specific area but unintelligible to those outside it. As has been noted in chapter 2, we also found that asking the FLP fellows to sit through classes in disciplines far removed from their own often had a remarkable effect; it served to "denaturalize" the practices and assumptions of their own fields and made them less likely to make unwarranted assumptions about what would be obvious to their students. But the most powerful experience of the nature of disciplines was created in the second week of the FLP seminar, when each of the fellows taught a model lesson to the group in which he or she sought to present the basic operations that were needed to overcome a bottleneck in his or her field. The fellows, who had bonded with the other members of the group in the first week of the program and been impressed with the intelligence of their colleagues, often found that instructors from other departments had as much difficulty as many of their own students did in overcoming bottlenecks (Middendorf 2004; Middendorf and Pace 2001, 2007).

Formally constituted faculty learning communities like the FLP, are a particularly effective means of sharing the decoding process. But less institutionalized forms of interaction can also be very valuable. Small groups of instructors who have encountered decoding can come together with others in the same area or across disciplinary lines to share their experiences with the process. They can observe classes in different fields to become more aware of particular demands in their own disciplines. They can interview one another; observe each other's classes; discuss strategies for modeling, practice, and assessment; and even collaborate on works in SoTL.

The impact of decoding on the experience of those engaged in collective investigations of teaching and learning has been visible on campuses throughout the world. Nowhere has the potential of such shared experience been more fully realized than at Mount Royal University in Canada, where instructors used decoding to respond to a wide range of challenges, ranging from the redesign of individual courses to the examination of cross-disciplinary programs (Miller-Young and Boman, forthcoming).

The Mount Royal group has gone beyond simply repeating the original FLP interviews that focused on making explicit the mental operations required in a single instructor's courses. They have rethought the frame in which these exchanges occurred and made them more collaborative. Each interviewee went over a transcript of his or her interview and wrote reflections that were shared with the group. In the process they not only forged more powerful links within their community, but also contributed a new model for decoding. Their description of the experience is worth quoting at length:

> The Decoding interview itself was also important in our functioning as a collaborative learning community and generating a climate of trust. Its structure not only gave us the necessary permission to push one another's thinking, but also did not allow us to settle for superficial answers to questions and required us to be self-disclosing and honest with one another. Since the purpose of the Decoding interview is, explicitly, to support the interviewee in better understanding her own thinking, the process—including the pushing—is inherently in the service of the interviewee's own learning, which also helps her to see the interviewers as collaborators. This was evident because, while each of us described the Decoding interview as somewhat difficult and uncomfortable, we also each demonstrated a willingness to admit to shortcomings or mistakes during our interviews. (Jennifer Petit, Victoria Calvert, Yasmin Dean, Judy Gleeson, Roberta Lexier, Melanie Rathburn, and Margot Underwood, forthcoming.)

The process described in this passage requires a sense of safety. To fully realize of the potential of decoding in such collaborative settings, individuals must make themselves vulnerable They must be able to admit that there are places in their courses where learning is not occurring optimally and that there are things about operating in their discipline about which they are not fully conscious. In some academic environments such admissions could later be turned against those participating in the process. If those involved in decoding are constantly looking over their shoulders, concerned about the consequences of revealing their own ignorance about parts of the teaching process, progress can be impeded.

Therefore, it is necessary to build safeguards into the process. On the most basic level it is important to have firm and explicit guidelines for what will be done with any tapes or transcripts of the interviews. Some of the dangers of self-revelation can also be minimized by creating cross-disciplinary groups, in which only one member of an academic unit takes part. In the FLP we avoided inviting two members of the same department to participate during the same year unless we had done extensive inquiries to confirm that the relationship between the two colleagues was such that both could feel comfortable with the process.

Regardless of the makeup of the group, a decoding investigation should only be undertaken when all involved in this endeavor recognize the importance of confidentiality and fully respect the value of their colleagues' willingness to make themselves vulnerable. There need to be very clear guidelines about what will be done with the results of the meetings, as well as explicit discussion about respecting the willingness of instructors to work in areas where they may not yet have clear answers.

Decoding and the Scholarship of Teaching and Learning

Those who have gone through the first six steps of decoding have already identified a learning problem, systematically explored the mental operations that students need to get past it, developed strategies for modeling and helping students practice these skills, considered emotional obstacles to the process, and assessed the results. In the process they have produced most of the elements needed for making the transition from scholarly teaching to the scholarship of teaching and learning. Not surprisingly, we have seen numerous instructors move directly from a decoding project to the production of their first academic papers or scholarly articles about teaching and learning. The effectiveness of this paradigm as a bridge to SoTL was made clear more than ten years ago with the publication of the original *Decoding the Discipline* volume (Pace and Middendorf 2004), in which most of the contributors were making their first foray into writing about teaching.

Such sharing does not, however, have to assume traditional forms of disciplinary presentation. There has been considerable debate within SoTL about the extent to which work in the field should explore new avenues for sharing ideas about teaching and learning. (See, for example, Bernstein 2002, 2008, 2010; Felten 2013; Woodhouse 2010.) Daniel Bernstein and Randy Bass have presented a particularly forceful expression of this possibility:

> We need to imagine new genres for sharing insights that are much broader than our current models for publishing. We need to develop much more interplay between product and process. The article-length study in a journal is a viable form of publishing that is especially appropriate for faculty focusing on a certain career path or seeking to share work that has matured. But that benchmark alone will not enable us to change professional practice on a broad scale. For the scholarship of teaching and learning to matter to many faculty, and for it to help transform teaching practices (and the quality of student learning), we need to conceptualize forms of "going public" built more on the idea of cycles of product and process, rather than on the linear line of traditional scholarship. And we need to make more robust use of digital tools and archiving resources to give faculty outlets for sharing their insights and resources. (2005, 43)

Mary Taylor Huber and Pat Hutchings have presented a catalog of venues for sharing SoTL outside of traditional publishing, including course portfolios, repositories of course materials, student work, data, multi-university meetings and initiatives, conferences, and workshops (2005, 27–28, 122–24). Decoding can be used in all of these contexts to share ideas and to provide a framework for making visible the systematic effort that goes into teaching. In tenure and promotion dossiers and in annual reports, for example, the steps of the decoding process can offer a context within which to make clearer to others the kinds of serious thinking that has gone into the revision of courses. This language can also be very effective in proposals for support for course development projects. And for those who are willing to go a step further, decoding can be the basis for portfolios that explore in greater depth the intellectual framework within which a course has been redeveloped and the specific steps that have been taken to increase learning (Bernstein 2002; Bernstein et al. 2006).

Thus, if those using the decoding process are to take proper advantage of its ability to transform teaching and learning, it will be necessary to make use of the full spectrum of presentations. As has hopefully been obvious in this book and in our other publications and conference presentations, the decoding approach can serve as the foundation for work that exploits traditional scholarly forms of communication. But our efforts to share these ideas have also included workshops at conferences and on university campuses that were much more interactive, often involving hands-on work and videos of interviews with faculty and students who have experienced decoding.

The sharing of ideas about decoding will hopefully be facilitated by our website (http://decodingthedisciplines.org/) where those exploring the paradigm will be able to share their efforts to identify bottlenecks and to make explicit the mental operations required in particular disciplines, subdisciplines, and cross-disciplinary areas. Users will be able to post a wide range of artifacts from their work, including videotaped interviews, class lessons designed to model or give practice on specific mental operations, the voices of students in the form of course-work or direct comments on the process, and a range of other artifacts. And scholars of teaching and learning will have access to a bibliography of publications based on decoding and to a listserv that will allow them to share announcements and opportunities for collaboration for conferences and publications.

Such virtual contacts will be augmented with face-to-face sharing of ideas about decoding at academic meetings, campus workshops, and special conferences devoted solely to the paradigm. It is hoped that the combination of traditional scholarly presentations, the direct experience of decoding in workshops, and the sharing of materials on the internet will strengthen the network of scholars of teaching and learning and scholarly teachers who are generating work in this area and putting it into practice in their courses.

Decoding on a Departmental Level

Thus far we have been considering ways in which the seventh step of the decoding process can be realized by sharing knowledge about teaching and learning that can be used in individual courses. But it can also serve as a foundation for collective enterprises that aim at larger changes in higher education. At the departmental level, decoding can help create a consensus about the problems faced by those teaching in the field and about the strategies that may be used to respond to these challenges. Too often, well-meaning efforts to rationalize the offerings of an academic unit collapse for the lack of a clear, shared vision of the nature of the problem. Decoding can provide a focus for such reconsiderations of departmental offerings.

A clear example of the realization of this potential was visible in January 2014 in South Africa, where the commercial law faculty of the University of the Free State met to decode a central task that creates great difficulties for many of their students—the reading of case law. Working with a shared example, they systematically reconstructed the steps they would each take to make sense out of this type of legal text. I served as an outside observer who could occasionally point out that their shared familiarity with the process had caused them to leave unopened a "black box" that might have the potential to mystify students.

After several hours of intense work, the group emerged with a series of clearly defined steps that were necessary for successfully reading examples of case law. To their surprise, on several occasions they discovered that different members of the group actually followed slightly different, but equally effective, paths through the maze of reading law. This further enriched their understanding of the learning process, since in the past their students may have become confused if they encountered diverse ways of operating in different courses without being told that these were equally valid approaches. When they completed this intense session, the faculty of the mercantile law division were most likely in a better position than their counterparts in any law school in the world to think collectively about the manner in which these mental operations should be introduced across the curriculum (Moolman, Wilkinson, and van Jaarsveldt, 2015).

Instructors in athletic therapy at Mount Royal University in Canada used decoding in a different way. The program was undergoing a major transformation in its curriculum and pedagogy, moving to a competency-based approach using scenarios or clinical cases as the foundation for teaching. To assist in this process, Michelle Yeo and Ron MacDonald from the university's Faculty Learning Community on Decoding the Disciplines interviewed five members of the athletic therapy team to make explicit those aspects of implicit practice in the field that were not being adequately conveyed to students. Transcripts of the interviews were read by all the participants and led to discussions that illuminated many aspects of the process the unit was engaged in. From these interactions there emerged a much greater sense of the need to focus on elements such as rethinking the relationship between academic learning and experience in the field, conveying the visual and kinesthetic knowledge that emerges in actual practice, and preparing students for the intense emotional pressures that often accompany decision making in this profession (Yeo et al. forthcoming).

Through processes such as this, decoding can make a major contribution to the solution of a problem that has long beset higher education: finding the basis for the creation of a rational curriculum. Traditional paths through college, organized almost entirely around content, have serious problems. Students are frequently subjected to haphazard training in which some skills are taught repeatedly and others are never modeled at all. Under such conditions instructors in advanced courses cannot count on all of their students having the skills necessary for work at that level. Moreover, course offerings organized around subject matter may not even be effective at conveying content if students lack crucial understanding of the mental operations needed to make sense of it. After going through the decoding process, for example, one scholar realized that most students never learned anything meaningful about a crucial field in his department simply because it was placed at the beginning of the march through the topics, at a point in the curriculum where very few of the students had mastered the skills necessary to really assimilate the issues.

In the past it has been very difficult to create effective sequences of courses when the only model of skills development was a vague notion of critical thinking. But decoding can provide much more effective criteria for such development. When there has been a major effort to identify the bottlenecks in a discipline and to define the mental operations that are needed to overcome these obstacles, those working in the field can construct course sequences based on the real needs of students. When these elements of learning are made explicit, it is clear that certain problem areas need to be addressed early in a program, since nothing in the field will make sense without overcoming these problems, and that other bottlenecks can be left until later in a students' career. In such an analysis those bottlenecks that are threshold concepts will be clear, and these can be dealt with at the appropriate time.

The potential for such an approach is evident in the work of the History Learning Project (HLP) at Indiana University (IU). As was noted in chapter 7, the HLP conducted extensive interviews with members of IU's Department of History, in which faculty identified common bottlenecks in their courses and were then pressed to delineate the mental operations needed to get past them. It quickly became clear that all of the necessary skills could not be taught simultaneously and that there needed to be some strategy for sequencing them.

Therefore, at a teaching retreat organized by my HLP colleague Arlene Díaz, the faculty and graduate students of the Department of History were presented with a set of bottlenecks common in our courses and with some of the mental operations needed to overcome them. Teams each took one of these skills and defined how it would be addressed at each level of our undergraduate curriculum (Shopkow 2010).

For example, the team assigned to map a response to the bottleneck involving primary sources decided that introductory (100-level) courses should ideally focus on helping students to recognize the difference between primary and secondary sources and to learn to pose basic questions about artifacts from the past (e.g., who created it, when and why it was created, what its audience was, etc.). At the 200 level, instructors would model and give students practice at understanding the processes by which such historical artifacts were created, the choices that were made in their production, and the intentions of their creators. At the 300 level, students would be challenged to evaluate the trustworthiness of sources to systematically compare different primary sources, and to begin to deal with issues of ambiguity and contradiction in these documents or artifacts. Finally, at the 400 level, students would be asked to develop relationships among multiple sources, to synthesize what can be learned from different sources, and to create their own historical interpretations (Díaz et al. 2008).

Such efforts can create a general blueprint for a department wishing to provide students with rational pathways through its course offerings. It is possible to indicate the level of complexity to be encountered at each stage of the program, thus allowing instructors to offer courses with appropriate challenges, knowing that more basic bottlenecks had been addressed at a lower level. This would present advisers and students with a better basis for deciding which courses were most appropriate, and majors would emerge with a solid grounding in the skills needed to think in the field.

In such departmental decoding sessions it is particularly important to consider issues of safety and confidentiality. As noted earlier in this chapter, successful decoding focuses on areas of difficulty, and the sharing of these could potentially have negative consequences for vulnerable instructors. Anyone proposing a shared decoding experience in a unit in which personnel decisions might be affected has an ethical responsibility to protect participants from such possibilities. Moreover, there is the practical fact that the decoding process simply will not work effectively unless everyone involved feels safe about acknowledging difficulties and sharing lack of experience. This is particularly important in departments in which teaching is divided among tenure-track and non-tenure-track faculty.

Bringing Students into the Decoding Process

In developing Decoding the Disciplines we have, of necessity, begun by focusing on certain aspects of the learning process and ignoring others. In chapter 8 we will explore some of the steps that might be taken in the future to expand decoding's vision of learning. But first it is important to acknowledge some of the steps that have already been taken to move beyond the narrow focus on faculty perspectives that has tended to dominate decoding so far.

In this respect the efforts of Peter Felten at Elon University are particularly promising. Under his guidance a group of very insightful undergraduates (Rachel Mehaffey, Julie Phillips, and Mary Rouse) were introduced to decoding, and they conducted interviews with instructors and other students to explore both groups' perceptions of bottlenecks and crucial disciplinary operations (Mehaffey et al. 2015). Students doing such research can bring important insights into the lived experience of other students, and they are often able to get more honest and complete responses from their peers. Moreover, involvement in such research can be transformative for the student researchers themselves, and their enthusiasm can motivate the students they are studying (Cook-Sather, Bovill, and Felten 2014). One hopes that the pathways being forged by Felten and his undergraduate colleagues will be followed up on other campuses. The relatively small role of student voices in decoding work thus far is a deficit that must be remedied.

At the other end of the higher education spectrum two FLP veterans at Indiana University, Leah Shopkow in history and Mimi Zolan in biology, have made decoding a central part of pedagogy courses that they offer to PhD students in their respective departments. Their students are prepared to being a career in university teaching with an understanding, not only of the content of their disciplines, but also with a grasp of the kinds of mental operations that students must master to understand it. The spread of such courses could have an immense impact on the future of academic teaching.

The Joy of Shared Decoding

It should be clear by now just how essential sharing is to carrying out the decoding process and to spreading the fruits of such labor. But there is another reason for including it: the joy that emerges from the experience. In many discussions of teaching and learning, too little attention is devoted to the psychological rewards instructors may reap. There is a deep satisfaction in working with others to decode common bottlenecks that is difficult to replicate when working on one's own, and this can provide the energy to press forward with this work even when institutional rewards are not immediately forthcoming. As we have seen, decoding provides a common language and a point of focus that greatly facilitates such interactions. It can help create bonds among instructors that empower them as teachers and as members of the community within which they work. It can lessen the sense of isolation that diminishes the professional experience of many instructors. And by reminding us of how crucial the task of education is for the societies in which we live, decoding can broaden the sense that we are part of a greater effort to improve the quality of life of those around us.

8. THE FUTURE OF DECODING

IF WE ARE to fully live up to our responsibility to the future, we must sometimes allow ourselves to dream. In imagining what might be possible someday, we sometimes discover what needs to be done in the present. Therefore, I invite you to join me in an exploration of the uses to which the Decoding the Disciplines process might be put in the future. It is, of course, impossible to predict with any accuracy just how the approach will be put to use. Decoding is a tool, and, like any other tool, it will be reshaped and used in ways that were never imagined by its original creators. Nonetheless, I cannot conclude this book without considering directions that the process might take in future years. There is inevitably something utopian in some of these speculations, but temporarily leaving behind the realm of the certain can free our way to begin working towards the possible. So let us dream for a few more pages.

The Limits of Decoding

Before plunging into speculations about the directions decoding might take in the future, it is important to consider once again the parameters and the limitations of the paradigm. Decoding is not an impersonal, technocratic solution to all learning problems. It does not eliminate the need to create a meaningful personal relationship with students. From the perspective of the instructor, there remain profound ethical issues about how one engages with students, and teaching is still a vocation in which the instructor's own personal voyage is not unrelated to the success he or she experiences in the classroom. The kinds of issues about the development of self-efficacy raised by scholars such as Marcia Baxter Magolda and Patricia M. King (2004) are only partly addressed in the efforts of decoding to maximize the internalization of academic ways of thinking. And, as Ken Bain has effectively reminded us in *What the Best College Students Do* (2012), issues of students' personal orientation to their own learning and of grit and determination must be considered. Such studies remind us that education should not be entirely reduced to the inculcation of disciplinary skills.

Nor does decoding take the place of research into the social factors that interfere with student learning. Student culture and the many inequities of contemporary society shape the experience of higher education in ways that may seriously interfere with the efficacy of the decoded classroom, and we need a great deal more anthropological, sociological, and historical research into the larger social framework within which instruction exists. Differences of gender, sexual orientation, social and economic status, religion, educational background, class, region, and nationality all shape the context within which learning occurs, and, while decoding may be useful in responding to some of these challenges, it cannot of itself bring us all the insights we need about the complex web of human relations that students bring to our courses.

Finally, there is a great deal of research into the biological foundations of learning that can benefit decoding but cannot be replaced by it. Like almost all educational theorists before us, we have worked entirely with what learning looks like from the outside. We have made guesses and tested hypotheses on the basis of student behavior. Yet as new knowledge emerges from neuroscience about how human brains process information, it will most likely be necessary to reexamine the ways in which we have defined bottlenecks in particular disciplines and some of the strategies for modeling, providing practice, assessing learning, and motivating students. As Mary Helen Immordino-Yang notes, "Neuroscientific evidence suggests that we can no longer justify learning theories that dissociate the mind from the body, the self from social context" (2011, 101). Again, decoding may provide a particularly useful framework for translating new insights into classroom practice, but it cannot be the sole source of such new forms of understanding.

New Directions for Using Decoding in Instruction

Within these limits, decoding is already providing a highly useful framework within which to respond to the challenges of the college classroom, and in the future the approach will most likely serve this goal in new ways. On the simplest level, it is easy to see how decoding could be applied to other areas of instruction. For example, throughout this work the term *classroom* has been used—primarily to avoid incessant repetition of the word *course*. But this usage is also a reminder that—to the best of my knowledge—decoding has not yet been systematically used in online courses. This is a serious omission, because the process could be particularly useful in helping instructors realize the potential of such new media for instruction.

The process of identifying common bottlenecks to learning and of defining required mental operations could provide a needed focal point in digital learning. Since much instruction in this area is designed before contact with a particular group of students, and since many forms of traditional feedback are missing, it is particularly important to target those aspects of a course that are most apt to be problematic. The attention to breaking global tasks into their component parts that is key to decoding, and its approach to practice and assessment are obviously very compatible with online instruction. In my own courses, many of these activities are already conducted asynchronously and at a distance. Translating the modeling step from the classroom to the internet would require more serious reconsideration, but there is no doubt that new strategies for this could be devised.

Several experiments with using the decoding process to increase the effectiveness of service learning point to another area in which the approach could be productively used. Working within this framework, Indiana University English professor Joan Linton identified certain patterns of listening as a crucial mental operation that her students need to master to effectively interact with groups in situations such as homeless shelters. To model these skills, she introduced them to the "yes–and" strategy from improvisational comedy and saw a marked improvement in student writing on their experiences. (For more on this exercise see Middendorf and Shopkow, forthcoming.) And a faculty learning community at Mount Royal University has systematically used decoding interviews to explore the issue of reciprocity, a crucial element in courses that involve college teachers, students, and community partners. From the literature on the topic and their own practice, they were aware that the coming together of these very different groups raised complex issues about roles and communication that were significantly different from those encountered in other types of classes and that there was even the possibility that these interactions could have a negative impact on community organizations. Therefore they began to unpack their own experiences with using service learning and community engagement through decoding interviews followed by self-study reflections. A systematic, qualitative analysis of the transcripts of the interviews was conducted that focused on the ways in which participants' understanding of reciprocity deepened (Miller-Young et al. 2015; Petit et al. forthcoming).

Decoding has helped challenge some of the assumptions that these instructors were making about the interactions between various groups involved in these projects at the same time that it allowed them to shift from working *for* community partners to working *with* them. They recognized more clearly steps they had been taking automatically in their interactions with the various stakeholders and were better able to evaluate whether these were really the most effective ways to operate. As one participant reported in her self-study, "It is one thing to write about your thoughts and to reflect on them, but it is something entirely different to have to explain your thoughts and be questioned on each detail. Participating in the decoding interview made me re-examine my own thinking and practice; it challenged me to think about myself and my beliefs" (Miller-Young et al. 2015, 39).

In addition to its application to different types of courses, decoding also naturally generates a host of other questions that can serve as the launching point for investigations into the scholarship of teaching and learning (SoTL). An increased awareness of the mismatch between disciplinary operations and student preconceptions—an awareness built into much decoding practice—automatically raises questions about the nature of the mental baggage that students bring into our classrooms. One could compare the effectiveness of various modeling or practice strategies, and there is certainly no shortage of research topics in the area of emotional bottlenecks. There are issues concerning the intersection of bottlenecks and gender, race, ethnicity, class, age, and other factors that shape student learning. One might, for example, study the kinds of bottlenecks that tend to create problems for certain categories of students or the effectiveness of specific forms of modeling for particular groups. And if the experience of Indiana University's History Learning Project (HLP) holds for other disciplines, as we expect it will, such interviews can lead to new understandings of the intersection of disciplinary epistemology and student experience.

Another issue that needs much more serious consideration is the role of students in the entire decoding project. Most of the work within the paradigm to date has focused on faculty perceptions of disciplinary operations. This has been an understandable and probably necessary focus, since there was so much to learn about the disciplines from the perspective of those who create knowledge in them. But it is also important to more systematically examine students' experience of bottlenecks and of modeling and practice exercises based on decoding.

The research by Elon University undergraduates described in chapter 7 has given us a glimpse into the complexity of student encounters with new models for operating within disciplines (Mehaffey, Phillips, Rouse, and Felten 2015). Their work points to the need for more systematic research into students' experience of bottlenecks and of the modeling strategies that we use to help them overcome these obstacles. We need to have more precise notions about the understandings of disciplinary work that students typically bring to the university. More study should to be devoted to the ways in which students respond to differences between their preexisting views of their disciplines and the procedures and subject matter that they encounter in their courses in particular fields. Again, the Elon example demonstrates the importance of actively engaging undergraduates— and it should be added PhD students—in this research. They can often capture student attitudes in ways that are difficult for more obvious authority figures. In future work in this area students will, hopefully, have a much larger role not only as the subject of more extensive analyses of their experience within scholarship of teaching and learning using the paradigm.

A closely related issue has been raised by my good friend Christian Briggs: the decoding of failure. We have remained focused throughout our work on the steps that lead to success in courses, but there is a structure to unsuccessful responses to the demands of a course, and more research is needed to understand the pathways to failure. This is particularly important because in their interviews with other undergraduates at Elon, Rachel Mehaffey, Julie Phillips, and Mary Rouse found that some of the students they talked with were actually able to articulate the mental operations that their instructors believed were effective in the discipline, yet they chose to pursue different paths in their own work in these courses. An analysis of these phenomena might either yield alternative routes to success or provide information about what caused students to choose less effective ways to respond to the challenges of the course. To get at such information one might replicate the Elon study on a larger scale, following a number of students across a semester to get more information about how efforts to present mental operations in decoded courses intersect with the behavior and understanding of different students and what consequences this has for success in a course.

Theory and Decoding

As Peter Felten has noted, the scholarship of teaching and learning in the United States "tends to be classroom-oriented, rather than theory- or hypothesis-driven. Faculty often start with 'a teaching problem' (Bass 1999), a discipline-based question linked to what they see in the learning, or the misunderstandings, of their own students" (Felten 2013, 121; see also Hutchings 2007) This pattern has, to a large extent, been visible in the early stages of decoding as we began with the practical issues that emerged in particular classrooms and then moved inductively to explore solutions to these problems. The inclusion of Arlene Díaz and Leah Shopkow in the HLP increased the theoretical dimension of decoding, particularly with Leah's exploration of the relationship between bottlenecks and disciplinary epistemology (Shopkow et al. 2013b). However, until recently decoding has generally remained focused on the solution to practical problems arising in student learning.

Now that the practical framework for decoding has been developed, it is time to link this work to broader philosophical, sociological, and psychological approaches. As noted in chapter 7, the Faculty Learning Community on Decoding the Disciplines at Mount Royal University has taken the interview process in new, more collaborative directions. But they have also moved beyond the consideration of individual interviews to systematically explore themes that were present in multiple interviews, devoting special attention to the presence of such patterns as the deconstruction and reconstruction of knowledge, pattern recognition, acceptance of the provisional nature of one's early encounters with a subject, expanding one's perspective on an issue as work progresses, paying active attention to cues in one's environment, taking initiative in the pursuit of knowledge, and being ethical and authentic in one's practice. They divided these into three large categories: ways of thinking, ways of practicing, and ways of being (Miller-Young and Boman, *Using the Decoding the Disciplines Framework*, forthcoming).

Even more striking has been the efforts of the group to bring new theoretical frameworks to bear on the decoding process. Ron MacDonald, for example, has focused on the role of identity in student learning, particularly in the professions. Focusing on interviews by instructors in nursing and journalism, MacDonald emphasizes the need for students to not only master a set of specific mental operations but also to assume the roles of professionals in the field they are entering. "The acquisition of professional disciplinary identities," he writes, "might usefully become a fully conscious process, a process reflected upon critically by its subjects, a process deconstructed and open to change by its subjects." To explore the nature of this necessary transfer of identity, MacDonald uses the narrative identity theory of Stuart Hall and the dialogical self theory of Hubert Hermans and Agnieszka Hermans-Konopka to suggest that the decoding interview might be expanded to systematically include the stories that professionals in the field use—consciously and unconsciously—to define and create their roles within their professions (MacDonald, forthcoming).

The Mount Royal group has also broadened our perspective on decoding by considering the process from various explanatory perspectives. In a very impressive article in the forthcoming issue, Genevieve Currie has used methods and insights from phenomenology to make visible the crucial aspects of the disciplinary practice revealed in the group's interviews. Within the transcripts Currie found evidence of "preflective" orientations these experts brought to the practice of their discipline that allowed them to be aware of and to make use of the experience flowing in. She makes explicit the role of bodily sensations in experts' practicing of their disciplines, and she points out the role of the lived experience of working in a field in creating expertise. Summing up the results of her analyses, Currie notes that the interviews

> illustrated that faculty had often learned the complexities and nuances within their disciplines over years and sometimes with a sensory response from their bodies. As educators we need to help students to pay attention to the noncognitive reactions they experience in learning our disciplines; the acquisition of embodied knowledge and pathic knowledge. We need to call attention with our students to our bodies and the experiential experiences in the lab and real world. . . . Within practice disciplines where we experience the world with types of knowledge related to touch, perceptions, feelings, actions and sensations, that cannot necessarily be translated back or captured in conceptualizations and theoretical representations, but nonetheless are modes of knowing, we need to give them expression and importance. (Currie, forthcoming)

In the same volume Michelle Yeo presents an alternative way of viewing the interview process, arguing that decoding has generally been conducted with "fundamentally cognitivist assumptions" and has focused on helping "experts unpack their own cognitive processes." She suggests, however, that many of the bottlenecks encountered in the interviews at Mount Royal "had more to do with ways of being-in-the-world, having affective, relational, and identity elements. In analyzing such transcripts, we argue that taking an interpretive rather than a strictly cognitive approach would seem to enrich the possibilities inherent in decoding work."

To take advantage of this aspect of the interview process, Yeo turns to hermeneutics, focusing particularly on German philosopher Hans-Georg Gadamer's *Truth and Method.* Decoding interviews, she argues, are very much like the kinds of dialogue that Gadamer believes are essential in the encounter with any text or with life itself. She therefore proposes enriching the cognitive focus of the decoding interview, which at times can have the effect of reducing the essence of expertise to a set of fixed mental operations, with "a surfacing of the hermeneutic concepts deeply present in the interviewees' descriptions of their work within their disciplines, revealing hermeneutic structures within the disciplines themselves."

Yeo examines a set of the Mount Royal interviews from this perspective, and explores from within the efforts of an acting teacher to find meaning in a script or journalism instructors' focus on "situatedness." She describes how they want their students to "step back from the constructed narratives to deeper questions of interpretation and meaning." The text of an interview becomes an entry point into the world of a nursing instructor who wants to explore with her students "the difficulty of *living* the code of ethics in practice, the complexity of the dilemmas nurses face that challenge their own pre-understandings (in Gadamerian terms)." In each case Yeo sees Gadamer's concern with dialogue both in the relationship between the instructor and the student and in her own relationship with the text of the interview itself.

Throughout her article Yeo seeks to remain in conversation with the text of the interviews, allowing herself to listen to the voices of the instructor-interviewees rather than imposing her own reality or values on their worlds of teaching. She argues, "A dialogic approach to the interviews, where the interviewer opens a space for the expert to descriptively explore and express their understandings . . . is paramount. This then requires the interviewer to put aside their own preconceptions and the 'historicity' of their own discipline." But she also sees the same "dialogic relationship" in the interactions of these instructors with their students (Yeo, forthcoming).

This brief description of the work of the Mount Royal University group fails to capture the richness of these scholars' analysis. But the depth of their analysis and the manner in which they challenge some of the ways that decoding has been conceptualized in the past are signs of the maturing of this work. It is quite possible that by focusing on mental operations we have de-emphasized important aspects of the lived experience of working within a discipline that students need to master. Beyond the question "How do you do that?" we may need to sometimes ask others: "What are you feeling in your body when you do that?" "How are you experiencing your environment at that moment?" "What kinds of ethical questions or conflicts are your considering when faced with that situation?" This does not mean that the cognitive issues that have been the focus of most previous decoding are irrelevant to student learning, but it does indicate that it would be prudent to explore other areas.

And it may be necessary to reconsider other assumptions that were made early in the development of the Decoding the Disciplines paradigm. At the outset we chose to use the term *discipline* provisionally and somewhat uncritically, as a kind of shorthand, in the belief that the investigation of generic critical thinking had already yielded most of the benefits that were available to that line of reasoning and that greater advances could now be made by focusing on learning in particular disciplines. But as a considerable body of analysis has made clear, this usage is problematic in two different ways. On the one hand, there may be significant differences within disciplines. As Nancy L. Chick has noted, the discipline of English includes at least four subdisciplines (literary studies, compositional studies, creative writing, and linguistics), each with its own approaches to teaching (2009, 39). Political science and anthropology provide equally striking examples of disciplines in which different sorts of courses may require radically different types of mental operations. Even within fields with less dramatic divisions, the mental operations required for success in different courses may vary considerably. Conversely, two courses in different disciplines may require the mastery of similar mental operations; historicized literary studies and history itself provide an obvious example. Finally, recent decades have been marked by a flood of interdisciplinary research and teaching that has washed away many disciplinary boundaries.

This problem of terminology obviously existed long before we began our work, but the process of decoding may itself contribute somewhat to the resolution of this confusion of boundaries in the future—at least in the realm of teaching. A systematic analysis of the mental operations in particular courses within a discipline should lay the basis for a more complex typology of learning in contemporary academia. We continue to find that it is best to begin a decoding analysis by burrowing deeply within particular fields of study rather than looking for common, overarching patterns. But, as the Mount Royal team has demonstrated, once the bottlenecks and the mental operations of a particular field are clearly identified, interesting patterns appear that are common to more than one discipline.

Thus, a systematic decoding of courses in a broad range of fields might produce a new map of teaching and learning in which old disciplinary frontiers are replaced by different patterns of similarities and differences defined by the bottlenecks and mental operations students actually encounter. Some instructors may find that the challenges they face have more in common with those encountered in other fields than with the learning issues that arise in the courses of colleagues in their own departments, and instructional alliances may develop that have relatively little to do with current institutional boundaries. The work of the HLP has revealed interesting parallels in some of the bottlenecks faced by students in courses in history and geology, two disciplines in which understanding developments over time is sometimes problematic. By contrast, some of the issues involving students' emotional resistance to the subject matter in particular history courses have much more in common with the challenges facing instructors in some other fields, such as political science, than they do with those in other history courses.

Institutionalizing Decoding within Academia

The full potential of decoding will most likely not be realized if its implementation remains on the level of the individual course and it is not made part of an effort to increase learning on a broader scale. As we have seen, the paradigm offers instructors a means of focusing their efforts and rationalizing the task of maximizing learning. But this is hard work that requires time, commitment, and insight. As such, it is difficult to imagine every instructor in a field—or even every department—individually going through the steps and finding new ways to help students get past bottlenecks. It is, however, not so difficult to envision research groups in particular disciplines doing much of this work for their colleagues; here the HLP provides at least a provisional model. Common cognitive and emotional bottlenecks in the field could be identified, the operations needed to surmount these obstacles could be explored, and strategies for modeling, practice, and assessment could be shared.

The impact of such efforts would be greatly increased, if they were supported through disciplinary organizations. Such institutional backing would greatly legitimize efforts to explore the common bottlenecks and mental operations that occur frequently within the courses in a particular field, and it would make the dissemination with the academic area much more effective.

It is essential that none of this be seen as prescriptive. The subject matter, the students, and the personalities of instructors, even within a single department, are much too diverse for one size to fit all. But the results of systematic investigations in decoding could open up a larger dialogue about teaching that is still relatively rare in academia today. This work could be presented, debated, critiqued, and improved through the same kinds of intellectual exchange as other disciplinary research—and, hopefully, in the same venues.

The impact of this work could also be greatly increased through the creation of materials that would make the results of decoding scholarship readily available to PhD students and new faculty. Ideally, an exposure to the results of decoding of specific disciplines by scholars throughout the world could be made a standard part of the education of PhD students, and new instructors could be provided with information about the most common bottlenecks in their disciplines and a wide range of specific responses to these pedagogical challenges from seasoned instructors. Plans for modeling, providing practice, and assessing particular skills, all created by experienced instructors, could be shared with those new to the work. No longer would new teachers have to re-create every bit of knowledge needed to be effective in the classroom, and their learning curve could be greatly improved.

Beyond the organization of decoding within disciplines, it is important to think about ways to provide social and institutional support for this work. It is to be hoped that our website will provide a space within which such work can be nurtured,[1] but other mechanisms may also need to be developed. A decoding interest group now exists within the International Society for the Scholarship of Teaching and Learning, and it will be hosting meetings at the conferences of the parent organization. An independent organization and international conferences on decoding may lie in the future, but that will have to wait until we see the reaction to the wave of publications on the paradigm that are scheduled to appear.

Decoding at an Institutional Level

Throughout this volume decoding has been discussed primarily in terms of its application on the level of the individual classroom, the faculty learning community or, at most, the academic department. But it could have an impact on the level of university administration as well. College deans and presidents face a host of problems that decoding can help solve.

Dan Bernstein, among others, has effectively argued that SoTL can be a very important asset to institutions of higher education by creating and spreading effective strategies for increasing student learning, generating processes of assessment, and furnishing evidence of faculty commitment to teaching (Bernstein 2013). It may in fact be argued, in the words of Mary Huber and Pat Hutchings, that "the scholarship of teaching and learning is an imperative for higher education, not a choice" (2005, 13).

Decoding can play a crucial role in realizing the potential of SoTL as a tool for helping achieve institutional goals. It can also provide criteria for evaluation, specific knowledge about student difficulties, criteria for planning curricula and advising, a shared language for mobilizing university initiatives, and a framework within which to address shared problems. All of this could make it an invaluable tool to university administrators trying to grapple with challenges that transcend the limits of the individual classroom or department.

One of the great issues that administrators must face is the problem of recognition and reward of teaching. If teaching is viewed as an entirely private and personal act, it is difficult to see how institutions are going to develop effective responses to ever more diverse students and ever more demanding subject matter. But this need often collides with the perception that it is impossible to make meaningful judgments about teaching—that research can be evaluated and teaching cannot.

Such notions ignore the fact that it took a century of hard work to produce such generally accepted institutions as established journals, the anonymous review, indexes of citations, and the outside reader in publishing, tenure, and promotion decisions, that create at least the impression of objectivity in research. This kind of cultural labor has only begun recently in the realm of teaching. The development of mechanisms like systematic peer review, course portfolios, and the institutionalization of SoTL has begun to address this imbalance, but we have far to go.

There remain, however, two potential problems in the use of SoTL in the structures of reward and recognition that exist in higher education. First, the complex situations that instructors face in the classroom and the strategies they develop to respond to them can be difficult to convey to others—particularly those outside the discipline. Scholars of teaching and learning are working to develop new languages for conveying this pedagogical complexity, but these are not yet generally recognized and appreciated by those outside the field. Second, traditional models of scholarly exchange—publications and conference presentations—do not match the needs of many instructors, who need to represent the work that they have done in their courses. The heavy professional responsibilities of many instructors make it difficult for them to undertake publishable studies in the scholarship of teaching and learning; they need a less formal mechanism for making visible their accomplishments.

Decoding can make an important contribution to resolving both of these difficulties. As we have seen repeatedly, the language of bottlenecks, mental operations, modeling, practice, emotional obstacles, and assessment can make the challenges and the strategies involved in teaching clear to those who have never come near the classroom in which they were originally manifested. The paradigm can serve as part of the rationale of teaching grants, tenure and promotion dossiers, and annual reports. Decoding thus has the potential to produce a kind of lingua franca that can be used in a variety of situations to make visible to outsiders the quality of an instructor's contribution to the educational goals of an institution.

Decoding can also be combined with some of the other alternatives to traditional scholarly forms discussed in chapter 7; in particular, it is easy to imagine a very productive merger of decoding with the teaching portfolio, a method developed by Dan Bernstein and others. Teaching portfolios provide a media for conveying the challenges faced in a particular course, the strategies developed to respond to them, and the results of these actions. They provide not only a detailed representation of the efforts of instructors to increase learning but also an opportunity for the review of instruction by scholars of teaching and learning at other institutions—thus adding the power of the outside reviewer to the decision-making process (Bernstein 2002; Bernstein et al. 2006; Hutchings 1998). The potential of using decoding as an intellectual and organizational framework with course portfolios is enormous, and the merger of the two approaches could create bodies of evidence that not only have an impact on the evaluation process but also serve to spread ideas about teaching and learning within an institution.

Decoding can also provide a basis for assessment and program review beyond the level of individual courses. We have seen too many examples of the ham-handed, top-down imposition of inappropriate norms and assessments at all levels and in many national contexts. But college administrators do need to respond to internal problems and to pressures from outside interests. If teachers fail to explain what they are about and the value of what they are doing, their vision of what should be happening in the classroom is bound to conflict with directives from university administration or, in many cases, national educational bureaucracies.

When a discipline has systematically decoded what it teaches, it is much easier to respond to requests (or, in many cases, demands) for evidence of student learning. Departments can explain clearly what are or are not appropriate forms of assessment in the discipline. And in many cases the assessments that have been created in individual courses as part of the decoding process can be assembled to provide a clear picture of how a unit is supporting learning, thus providing faculty with a real stake in the process (Hutchings 2011) at the same time that it maintains a focus on fundamental learning goals.

Greater knowledge of bottlenecks to learning and the basic mental operations that students must master to succeed in certain courses could also greatly rationalize the processes of advising and of curricular development. This is particularly true in the United States, where anarchy has generally followed the collapse of the traditionally rigid, subject-based curriculum of the 1960s. The diversification of knowledge itself, turf wars among academic units within universities over numbers of students, justifiable demands for a more diverse vision of the human experience, and a host of other factors have often left students— and in many cases their advisers—to face a chaos of course offerings with no clear criteria about what is required for success.

It is possible to imagine a different academic universe in which units systematically decoded their offerings and provided some indication of what level of mental operations might be required in each. Once departments clarify which of these operations are prerequisites for particular courses and which are actually taught, advisers would finally be in a position to place students in appropriate classes.

Information about what is really required in courses and what kinds of mental operations should be modeled in each could also become the basis for much more coherent decisions about curriculum. Rather than being based purely on subject matter, prerequisites and curricula might focus on a knowledge of what mental operations students must master to function in a class and, eventually, in their roles as professionals, citizens, and individuals. Decoding is uniquely positioned to provide the basis for such a rationalization of the curriculum because it can generate a shared language about learning that allows communication across specialties.

There are many other areas in which academic institutions could use decoding to develop responses to the challenges they face. Groups of faculty and educational developers, perhaps along with staff, administrators, and students, could use the decoding process to create better responses to shared problems, just as the group at Mount Royal University explored common strategies for assuring reciprocity in service learning and community engagement. My colleague Joan Middendorf has begun to explore such applications of decoding to institutional issues that transcend individual disciplines, and has brought together groups of instructors from different fields who share a common concern with diversity issues or sustainability. Each of these faculty learning communities has explored the mental operations that students must master to deal effectively with the issue at hand; considered ways to model, to create opportunities for practice, and to assess these skills; and devoted special attention to emotional bottlenecks.

It is possible to imagine such faculty learning communities using decoding to deal with a wide range of the challenges faced by their institutions. Issues such as race and cultural diversity, math anxiety, statistical reasoning, and professional ethics may emerge in courses in a variety of departments and have impacts on the life of a university that go beyond the curriculum of individual departments. Interdisciplinary groups could use decoding to explore the bottlenecks to learning in each area and develop strategies for helping instructors get past them. In some cases they may find that similar ways of operating are required in more than one field and be able to share in the development of common ways to help students grasp these. In other situations they might discover that disciplines have different ways of responding to an issue and focus on helping students make the transition from one disciplinary framework to another. Whatever the configuration, a systematic exploration of the bottlenecks preventing students from dealing with a particular issue can lay the groundwork for real breakthroughs in learning that could then be shared with colleagues across the institution.

A similar process could be employed to develop more effective ways to bring first-generation college students or international students into the world of the university. Unlike most decoding work, which concentrates on the learning problems of all students who are having difficulty in a particular course, here groups of faculty and perhaps administrators would focus on the problems faced by a group of students across many courses. In interviews with such students and with their instructors, it should be possible to systematically examine the preconceptions about the nature of college that students who are less familiar with a college environment typically bring to the university and to identify the steps that they use to pick courses, schedule work, seek help, and perform other essential tasks. Special attention would need to be paid to the emotional bottlenecks that commonly create problems for such students and to consider the preconceptions that help create mismatches between student expectations and what is really required for success in the world of higher education. Then decoding steps 3 through 6 could be used to help more students internalize those approaches that are most likely to lead them to a successful university career.

The decoding process can also be of great assistance in helping institutions make decisions about the use of new technologies for increasing student learning. It has become a cliché to assert that technological innovations should be implemented because they represent a better way to help students overcome particular difficulties and not just because a new technology has become available. Yet while such a position is quite defensible in itself, it rests on the assumption that we automatically know where the problem areas are and what students need to do to succeed at these tasks—assumptions that, as we have seen, are often very questionable. However, once the bottlenecks have been identified and the necessary mental operations defined, one can begin to make solidly grounded decisions about how technology can be used. A university operating on this basis would be in a much better position to make efficient decisions about the acquisition of new systems and to integrate them seamlessly into instruction.

With the best will imaginable, this kind of restructuring of academic procedures and priorities would be very demanding and, given the political and institutional framework of most universities, it may be utopian to imagine that it could be implemented everywhere. But institutions have a very great incentive to give it a try. Even if one were oblivious to the enormous cost of failure to individual students and to the broader society that desperately needs educated workers and citizens, the institutional needs of universities today call out for new ways to operate more efficiently in such areas as student retention. The inability to retain students has enormous practical costs for colleges and universities through the loss of tuition, the reluctance of students to enter universities where failures rates are high, and the displeasure of outside stakeholders. An institution that uses decoding to get a better understanding of what it is actually trying to teach might have a real competitive advantage, one that could carry real weight with governmental or private funders.

Decoding at the Interface between the University and the Broader Society

Despite lingering fantasies of the ivory tower, universities have never existed wholly outside society. Now, perhaps more than ever before, they are being asked to justify their existence in terms of values that are intelligible to those outside academia. Universities will ignore such requests at their own peril, and it is possible that decoding could have a role here as well. Some of the most ambitious efforts to bridge universities and their stakeholders have been generated within the Tuning movement. This initiative, which began with efforts of the European Union to coordinate the offerings of universities in member nations, has spread across the globe and sparked serious efforts to define the value added by various academic programs and disciplines. (See, for example, Kehm 2010; Marshall, Kalina, and Dane 2010.) A particularly promising manifestation of Tuning has been visible within university history departments in the United States, where this model is used as a means of drawing instructors into a discussion of teaching, creating a rational curriculum, and explaining the value their discipline has to potential employers and to society as a whole. To support such efforts the American Historical Association, with support from the Lumina Foundation, has generated a list of competencies that students can gain from history courses, and this list often serves as a template for departments reconsidering their teaching missions (Brookins 2012; Grossman 2012; Hyde 2012; Murphree 2013).

Such efforts are very encouraging, and could have a real impact both on organizing the teaching mission of departments and on making what academia is adding to society visible to outside stakeholders. But from the perspective of decoding there is one great weakness in the Tuning project. It begins with definition of core competencies and learning outcomes that can be gained from work in particular disciplines. Yet, as has been made clear throughout this book, it is dangerous to assume that the lists of skills that academics spontaneously generate automatically capture the essence of work in the field.

It is, however, possible to imagine a merger of the goals of Tuning with the methodology of decoding. The kinds of interviews described in chapter 2 could be used to make explicit the basic mental operations being cultivated in students, and these could be used to generate more complete inventories of the competencies that particular disciplines can bring to students and to society as a whole. Such a process could help make it clearer to the general public that a modern, functioning society requires a broad university curriculum for its continued existence. Ideally, collaboration between Tuning and decoding could expand the popular vision of the value of higher education to include contributions beyond the narrowly vocational criteria that are often dominant in current discussions. So long as we try to sell higher education in terms of subject matter, the value of much that occurs in academia will be difficult to explain. The value of knowing something about Old English literature or the anthropology of New Guinea is very difficult for the general public to understand, but the mental operations that underlie such studies have uses that can be presented much more easily to those who are skeptical about the value of a university education. Decoding has the potential of unearthing the real value added to society in even the most esoteric of subjects. It can provide us both with an example of the commitment of universities to the education of all students and a language in which to better explain how that education benefits the larger world.

Decoding and K–12 Education

Decoding could also be used to develop a new language of teaching and learning that would lessen the negative impact of the current dysfunctional chasm between secondary and higher education. A great deal of energy in our educational systems is currently wasted because those teaching at the college level have often not done a very good job of conveying to their counterparts at the primary and secondary levels a precise understanding of the kinds of mental operations that students will need when they enter colleges or universities. As a result, college instructors often have to spend a good deal of their time undoing what their students have been taught at the K–12 levels. Once a discipline has been carefully decoded, and the basic mental operations required for success in the field are made available, teachers in primary and secondary schools will have a much clearer target in their preparation of future college students.

There is, of course, no reason that the decoding model has to remain entirely within the realm of the university The focus on cognitive and emotional bottlenecks, modeling, practice, and assessment is relevant to all levels of education. There would probably need to be some adjustment to the process of defining disciplinary skills, since the great majority of teachers at the primary and secondary levels are not actively producing research in their fields. But this obstacle could easily be overcome through the sharing of ideas and experience between teachers and disciplinary specialists in a free and equal atmosphere in which the expertise of all parties is fully acknowledged and appreciated.

An important step in this direction has already been taken by my HLP colleagues Arlene Díaz and Leah Shopkow. In a course for future social studies teachers, they used decoding to understand and address the bottlenecks to learning that threatened to prevent their students from grasping the essence of history. In the process they were able to detect significant problems in two areas. The first involved the students' often simplistic understanding of history itself. Many of them needed "to move from seeing history as a fixed, single-stranded narrative created by historians gathering indisputable facts to seeing history as something created by historians as part of a contested intellectual discourse in which narratives and perspectives simultaneously satisfy disciplinary notions of truth and are in competition with each other" (Díaz and Shopkow, forthcoming). The second involved reconceptualizing their roles as history teachers; specifically, they noted the need to move beyond viewing their task as one of presenting a single narrative for students to memorize.

After working to provide students with a more complex vision of history and history teaching, Arlene and Leah systematically assessed the results, using pre-

and postcourse questionnaires, a multiple-choice diagnostic survey, and an analysis of the lesson plans that the students produced. They found that students' understanding of both the nature of history and of what they would need to do as teachers themselves improved across the semester, and that the quality of their lesson plans, as independently judged by several historians, was positively correlated with the sophistication of their understanding of historical reasoning. While the authors point out that the sample size of this study is small, it does offer some support for the notion that systematically introducing future history teachers to the mental operations that scholars perform in the study of history can help them to more effectively present the field to K–12 students. Hopefully this excellent study will be only the beginning of a larger effort to use decoding to help future secondary school teachers learn how to better prepare students for college work.

Decoding Education beyond the Academy

The unprecedented rate of increase in knowledge acquisition in our era has so altered the nature of learning that the concept of a university education may now seem antiquated. The ancient model of training in one's youth and of the application of that knowledge throughout one's prime is clearly not sufficient in a world in which technology, knowledge, and roles are changing within a time scale of months, not centuries. It is important, however, to recognize that this does not represent the end of a need for institutions of higher education. Learning how to learn requires intense and sustained training of the sort that universities are potentially quite effective at producing. The kind of education that is required represents far more than a simple transfer of data from one mind to another. We need to share not just the latest information but also the skills, techniques, procedures, ethical principles, personal dispositions, and—most important—wisdom that emerges from our collective encounter with the world; and the college classroom provides a particularly effective site for such complex cultural transmission.

Nonetheless, it is clear that complex learning will increasingly be taking place in many locations outside the university. An enormous amount of education already occurs within for-profit and nonprofit corporations; traditional on-the-job training programs have morphed into gigantic and complex educational systems that are quite independent of traditional higher education. Yet even this process has proven to be too rigid and inflexible for much of the learning that needs to occur, and groups like the Mozilla Foundation have begun to explore the creation of a system of badges that serve to certify competence in particular areas.

There is every reason to imagine that much of the decoding process outlined in this book can be as useful in these realms as it is in the formal institutions of higher education. Those involved in educational systems outside the university or in creating badges face many of the challenges that have been considered in the earlier chapters of this book, and the responses developed through decoding are often directly applicable. Bottlenecks, mental operations, modeling, practice, emotional blocks, and assessment can be as relevant in many forms of workplace education as they are in the academy. With few modifications, the decoding process could be employed in such situations to great effect.

Decoding and the Pedagogy of Everyday Life

We live in an extraordinarily rich era. The level of both practical and theoretical problem solving that is occurring around us every day is unprecedented. Yet as we each gain more and more understanding in limited fields we grow apart. It is as if our civilization has built not a single Tower of Babel but a vast city of such towers. We no longer speak the same language. The expertise that allows us to do extraordinary things also isolates us from one another; knowledge becomes a lonely possession, and the more that we build, the farther apart we drift.

It is not surprising that this problem should appear most prominently in the modern university. Here more than almost anywhere else, knowledge is piled on top of knowledge, and there is enormous pride in such a construction. The role of the university as an educational institution, however, also makes visible the tension between expertise and communication. Paradoxically, the very thing that makes instructors valuable to students—the richness of the knowledge and experience that they have accumulated—also makes it difficult for learners to take advantage of this knowledge.

Yet, while this paradox is foregrounded by the twin functions of the university system—to create knowledge and to share it—the situation outside academia is not very different. Expertise is everywhere. The kinds of academic skills that my colleagues and I have been trying to capture and share for many years are only an infinitesimal sample of the skills and knowledge possessed collectively by humanity. There is, most likely, not a conscious human being on the planet who does not have knowledge about how to function in the world that would be of some value to others in certain situations. Solutions to so many of the challenges we face every day have already been discovered, sometimes by people that we pass everyday on the street. But these responses are ordinarily not available to us. Like the traditional professor who struggles to resolve learning issues that have long been dealt with by his or her colleague in the next office, we are all trapped in that metaphorical classroom, unable to gain access to the answers that lie so close to us but seem beyond our reach.

The need for learning is present everywhere, and it is rapidly accelerating. The consumer faced with a new version of a computer application, the small business owner confronted with a shift in markets, the nonprofit director dealing with a newly emerging social need, the parent-to-be grappling with the implications of new information about fetal development or nutrition, the citizen having to decide which candidate's proposal for dealing with an environmental threat is most reasonable: all of these individuals need to learn and to learn fast.

There has been an impressive effort to respond to this demand for learning. Historians looking back at our era may well be struck by the proliferation of ways to acquire knowledge that we are generating in response in the challenges of everyday life. Individuals in the past generally had to create solutions to practical problems on their own or wait until they happened on someone with the requisite knowledge. Now, in a remarkably diverse range of situations, they have at their disposal a vast array of learning opportunities: how-to books, websites, YouTube videos, professional consultants, webinars, workshops, podcasts, listservs, FAQ pages, and a host of other media serve to pass practical knowledge and professional wisdom on to those in need of it.

We are all, thus, taking part in a vast experiment in decentralized education. A doctor or lawyer discussing a situation with a client, a drug company preparing instructions for a new medication, or an employer introducing new workers to the procedures of a company are all engaged in microteaching. But, like the traditional college professor, they are generally acting out folk traditions of teaching and learning that have never been subjected to systematic analysis They are often trapped within the language of their own expertise, unable to bridge the communication gap between themselves and those who most need their knowledge. We need to create a pedagogy of everyday life that can give greater focus and effectiveness to such moments of learning. Decoding may be able to provide the inspiration for such a practical pedagogy.

In most of these situations it will not be appropriate to simply transfer the seven steps in a mechanical fashion. Decoding the Disciplines came into being in the context of particular institutional possibilities and constraints that would often not be present in other situations. College instructors generally interact with students over a period of months, have the potential (if problematic) incentive of grades, and have a complex institutional framework to support their efforts. But they also are dealing with individuals who often do not see any real, immediate, personal gain from what a course has to offer. Those sharing expertise outside academia are often operating in different contexts where time frames are short and the immediate gains from learning are more visible. Thus, the applicability of insights gained from college teaching to many other situations would have to be considered on a case-by-case basis.

On a deeper level, however, the day-to-day situations these teachers find themselves in are not so different from those that have been considered throughout this book: computer programmers writing up instructions for end users, or experienced fund-raisers trying to explain their strategy to the directors of a new nonprofit are facing many of the same challenges posed to university professors. Each group is so immersed in its own knowledge that it finds it difficult to understand why others cannot see what seems so obvious. And each must find some way to deal with most or all of the elements in the decoding paradigm.

It is thus important to go back to the initial problem posed by decoding and to explore the development of new approaches that will produce equivalent processes for identifying the skills of experts and sharing them as effectively as possible with others. An effort in this direction has, in fact, been launched: the Choir Project, which I have had the opportunity to assist, has been experimenting with capturing a wide range of everyday expertise and making it available to the general public. It has begun to videotape individuals who have special skills ranging from graphic design to performing music for five-year-olds. Each of these people has solved some set of problems in the world, but unless there is an attempt to capture what he or she has learned, such solutions may never reach others who could benefit from them. The Choir Project processes these interviews, isolates the basic moves that are being made, and makes the information available on its website.[2]

Some of challenges faced by these everyday experts are quite practical: how to manage a set of highly skilled introverts or how to respond to the problem of stage fright. But there is also a deeper wisdom that emerges from these conversations, as when the manager of a company designed to support start-ups discusses the need to embrace the possibility of failure or when a computer programmer shares strategies for listening to coworkers talk about their experiences with depression.

While the processes used and the products produced by the Choir Project are significantly different from those involved in decoding higher education, the initiative is responding to the same general problem. It is imagining a world in which a wide range of techniques are developed to more systematically capture the skills, knowledge, and wisdom of experts in many fields and to pass these on to others as seamlessly as possible.

The potential of systematically sharing the skills and wisdom of everyday experts is enormous. It can provide a resource to individuals who are facing a particular challenge—for example, a parent who is trying to decide how to deal with a child's access to technology or a designer who is trying to translate an abstract idea into a tangible graphic. But it can also reveal habits of the heart that can be captured and made available to others on a scale rarely contemplated before. It can offer at least partial answers to questions about what happens when people experience empathy and what it means to have a sense of citizenship. And it can bring us a new appreciation of the wisdom that lies hidden in people all around us.

The Intangible Benefits of Decoding

The towers of knowledge described in the previous section are lonely places. They separate us from one another and keep us from communicating about things that we care deeply about. And they prevent us from fully appreciating the often remarkable vision of other people. Throughout this book I have concentrated on the positive outcomes of the Decoding the Disciplines process for students, instructors, and society as a whole. As we have seen in these pages, decoding has enormous potential for assisting learning, either directly through its application in higher education or indirectly through the inspiration of parallel initiatives in other areas. But there is a secondary benefit to this cultural project: the impact of decoding is not limited to those whose learning is aided. It also can be a transformative experience for those of us who do the decoding, as well, providing them an opportunity to escape the silos of their own expertise and find a space where we can meet those who are very different from ourselves.

Decoding was created as a means of facilitating the flow of skills, knowledge, and wisdom across the chasm separating teacher and student. At its core, it is about communication and translation. The process begins with a decision to listen as closely as possible to the words of experts and then to seek out a space in which they can really meet with novices. But this also requires a deeper level of communication between those doing the decoding and the experts—and, by extension, between instructors and students. There must be an acceptance of the other and a willingness to temporarily abandon the armor of one's own expertise and to enter into a kind of creative ignorance. And—like any successful act of communication—when it works, decoding changes both the parties in the interaction. There is a coming together, and a lessening of the sense of isolation that always lurks somewhere in the human consciousness.

The systematic exploration of the knowledge and the practices of another human being takes one into a different mental universe, as decoders experience the wonder of sameness and difference that makes our species so interesting. Fields of endeavor that have been ignored or even dismissed as uninteresting suddenly open up in all their complexity. The world is seen from a slightly different angle, and from that perspective new possibilities emerge. Solutions to life problems appear in the most unexpected places. But, just as important, the process can also help us gain new appreciation for those who have devised these solutions, even when they are quite different from ourselves. It can create a deeper sense of the value of the otherness of another human being. Each of us can only realize a tiny part of the spectrum of human possibilities, and decoding can help us appreciate those qualities that we ourselves have not cultivated. It can remind us that, as members of this particular species, we are all involved in a great task of self-realization that exceeds the capacity of any one of us to fully comprehend. It can bring us back to the realization that we are all students just as we are all teachers.

 **EPILOGUE**

FOR YEARS I have believed that watching a well-run preschool is one of the best ways to understand how to maximize learning in a college class. Here it is easy to observe in its most basic form the subtle channeling of students' natural energy, the creation of challenging tasks that carry them to new levels of learning, and the adjustment of teachers to the needs of their students. All of this can be not only an inspiration but also an antidote to academic teaching traditions that have sometimes stifled the natural creativity of students, repeated the tired rituals of instruction, and assumed that students must always adapt to the assumptions and convenience of their instructors.

Thus it is, perhaps, not surprising that the final piece of this book would occur to me while lying on the floor in the first and second grade classroom of Claudio Buchwald in the innovative Harmony School in Bloomington, Indiana. For many months I had been attending a weekly Feldenkrais class that happened to use that room. The space itself was dense with evidence of learning. Students' art work and intellectual productions were everywhere, but there were also subtle—and sometimes not so subtle—visual stimuli for reinforcing previous learning and for introducing students to new concepts. The signs on the walls marking the cardinal directions were only the most obvious tools integrating learning into a lived environment. Virtually every object in the room served a teaching function but, more important, they all functioned together to create a world in which it was more natural to learn than not to learn.

In that moment on the floor I realized that this was the ideal toward which Decoding the Disciplines had been evolving. We had originally conceived of decoding as a series of specific interventions to respond to individual bottlenecks to learning, but over time a different possibility has emerged. The attention to problem areas in learning continued, as did the emphasis on making explicit and teaching the mental operations that students must master to get past these bottlenecks. But rather than limiting this process to a discrete set of pedagogical moves, it had become possible to imagine a college course in which every element was structured around making these mental operations part of a learning environment within which students lived during their semester's sojourn. Every aspect of a course, from the format of the syllabus, to the classroom activities, lectures, and discussions; to quizzes, exams, and papers; to visual images, the choice of examples, and conversations outside class; and even to the first words uttered by the instructor when the students enter the classroom: all of these would be shaped by an awareness of the need to help students master a few central mental operations.

In such an environment, learning ideally would be naturalized. Students would move toward mastery with the same ease that raindrops eventually find their way to the ocean. It would require active resistance to avoid such learning. There would, of course, be those students who had an internal need to resist the process as part of a continuing adolescent revolt, the need to invest their energy in other aspects of their lives, or distrust of the worldview embedded in the field. But these would be the exception. Any student who had the most basic requirements for college work and was willing to make a commitment to be involved in the course would be drawn by a kind of pedagogical gravity toward the core of the discipline.

This is, of course, a dream. But it is a goal toward which we can work, even if we know that it will never be entirely achieved. This vision can provide a shared mission to draw students into the world of learning by pooling the efforts in classrooms around the world. It can offer us a context within which to bring together the insights and techniques that are being generated by scholars of teaching and learning and by researchers in education and psychology. It can help us to fulfill the mission of higher education in a world in which complex thinking is required of everyone and to explain that mission to those outside our institutions. And it help erode some of the disparities in learning opportunities that contribute so greatly to the inequalities and injustices of our world while offering a place at the table of knowledge to many who are currently excluded.

Notes

Introduction

1. The problematic nature of the concept of academic disciplines will be discussed in chapter 8.

1. Finding the Bottleneck

1. From the beginning of our work we have been aware of the potentially problematic nature of the term *discipline,* but given its deep roots in the structure of academia and its general correspondence to the kinds of thinking required of students in courses in different departments, we have used the term provisionally. For a discussion of the need to unpack this concept, see chapter 8. Moreover, as will be made clear in chapters 7 and 8 decoding may also be employed outside the context of a single discipline.

2. It should be noted that even in this example what seems to be a relatively trivial problem (citation form) may result from a deeper misunderstanding of the nature of knowledge creation in the discipline (i.e., its epistemology). It is possible that a more thorough modeling of this process might help students grasp other essential aspects of operation in the discipline. Nonetheless, in most cases an instructor would probably be able to find more effective bottlenecks to work on.

3. Modeling Operations

1. My colleague Joan Middendorf first recognized the importance of metaphors in decoding, and she and Leah Shopkow will be exploring this aspect of the practice more thoroughly in "Decoding the Disciplines: How to Help Students Learn Critical Thinking" (2016).

4. Practice and Feedback

1. The compatibility of decoding and JiTT is not entirely a matter of chance. Gregor Novak generously gave presentations on JiTT to the fellows of the Freshman Learning Project during the program's summer seminars. In the process we were influenced by JiTT techniques, and Novak became aware of decoding. While the two approaches began independently, as they developed there was a good deal of productive interaction.

5. Motivation and Emotional Bottlenecks

1. It should be noted that this example represents only the very beginnings of Erkan and Smith's work and that they have since moved to the forefront of thinking about the use of digital evidence to reveal student thinking.

6. Assessment

1. Beyond the Bubble, http://beyondthebubble.stanford.edu/.

8. The Future of Decoding

1. See the Decoding the Disciplines website, http://decodingthedisciplines.org/.
2. The Choir Project, http://www.choir.com.

References

Allen, Deborah E., Richard S. Donham, and Stephen A. Berngardt. 2011. "Problem-Based Learning." *New Directions for Teaching and Learning* 128: 21–29.

Allitt, Patrick. 2005. *I'm the Teacher, You're the Student: A Semester in the University Classroom.* Philadelphia: University of Pennsylvania Press.

Angelo, Thomas, and K. Patricia Cross. 1993. *Classroom Assessment Techniques: A Handbook for College Teachers.* San Francisco: Jossey-Bass.

Ardizzone, Tony, Fritz Breithaupt, and Paul C. Gutjahr. 2004. "Decoding the Humanities." In *Decoding the Disciplines: Helping Students Learn Disciplinary Ways of Thinking,* edited by David Pace and Joan Middendorf. *New Directions in Teaching and Learning* 98: 45–56.

Bain, Bob. 2006. "Rounding Up Unusual Suspects: Facing the Authority Hidden in the History Classroom." *Teachers College Record* 108(10): 2080–2114.

Bain, Ken. 2012. *What the Best College Students Do.* Cambridge, MA: Harvard University Press.

Bain, Kenneth, and Randy Bass. 2012. "Threshold Concepts of Teaching and Learning That Transform Faculty Practice (and the Limits of Individual Change)." In *Transforming Undergraduate Education: Theory That Compels, Practices That Succeed,* edited by Donald W. Hayword, 189–207. Lanham, MD: Rowman and Littlefield.

Barr, Robert B., and John Tagg. 1995. "From Teaching to Learning—A New Paradigm for Undergraduate Education." *Change: The Magazine of Higher Learning* 27(6): 13–26.

Barton, Keith C. 2008. "Narrative Simplifications in Elementary Students' Historical Thinking." In *Researching History Education: Theory, Method, and Context,* edited by Linda Levstik and Keith C. Barton, 183–208. New York: Routledge.

Bartholomae, David. 1986. "Inventing the University." *Journal of Basic Writing* 5(1): 4–23.

Bass, Randy. 1999. "The Scholarship of Teaching: What's the Problem?" *Inventio: Creative Thinking about Teaching and Learning* 1(1). https://my.vanderbilt.edu/sotl/files/2013/08/Bass-Problem1.pdf.

Bass, Randy, Maggie Debelius, Eddie Maloney, Nathaniel Rivers, and Norma Tilden. 2011. *Thresholds of Writing Project: Integrating Threshold Concept Theory with a Writing in the Disciplines Curriculum Development Approach. Georgetown University Project Progress Report 2011–2012.* https://assessment.trinity.duke.edu/documents/ThresholdsofWritingProjectFinal2011-FinalReport.pdf.

Bernstein, Dan, and Randy Bass. 2005. "The Scholarship of Teaching and Learning." *Academe* 91(4): 37–43.

Bernstein, Daniel. 2002. "Representing the Intellectual Work in Teaching through Peer-Reviewed Course Portfolios." In *The Teaching of Psychology: Essays in Honor of Wilbert J. McKeachie and Charles L. Brewer,* edited by Stephen F. Davis and William Buskist, 215–29. Mahwah, NJ: Erlbaum. https://kuscholarworks.ku.edu/handle/1808/7987.

———. 2008. "Peer Review and Evaluation of the Intellectual Work of Teaching." *Change: The Magazine of Higher Learning* 40(2): 48–51.

———. 2010. "Finding Your Place in the Scholarship of Teaching and Learning." *International Journal for the Scholarship of Teaching and Learning* 4(2). http://digitalcommons.georgiasouthern.edu/ij-sotl/vol4/iss2/4.

———. 2013. "How SoTL-Active Faculty Members Can Be Cosmopolitan Assets to an Institution." *Teaching and Learning Inquiry* 1(1): 35–39.

Bernstein, Daniel, Amy Nelson Burnett, Amy Goodburn, and Paul Savory. 2006. *Making Teaching Visible: Course Portfolios and the Peer Review of Teaching.* San Francisco: Jossey-Bass.

Bernstein, Jeffrey. 2012. "Plowing Through Bottlenecks in Political Science." In *The Scholarship of Teaching and Learning in and across the Disciplines,* edited by Kathleen McKinney, 74–92. Bloomington: Indiana University Press.

Beyer, Catharine Hoffman, Edward Taylor, and Gerald M. Gillmore. 2013. *Inside the Undergraduate Teaching Experience: The University of Washington's Growth in Faculty Teaching Study.* Albany: State University of New York Press.

Boman, Jennifer, Genevieve Currie, Ron MacDonald, Janice Miller-Young, Michelle Yeo, and Stephanie Zettel. Forthcoming. "Overview of Decoding across the Disciplines." In *Using the Decoding the Disciplines Framework for Learning across Disciplines,* edited by Janice Miller-Young and Jennifer Boman. *New Directions for Teaching and Learning,* forthcoming.

Boman, Jennifer, and Janice Miller-Young. Forthcoming. "Learning from Decoding across Disciplines and within Communities of Practice." In *Using the Decoding the Disciplines Framework for Learning across Disciplines,* edited by Janice Miller-Young and Jennifer Boman. *New Directions for Teaching and Learning,* forthcoming.

Bransford, John D., Ann L. Brown, and Rodney R. Cocking, eds. 2000. *How People Learn: Brain, Mind, Experience, and School.* Expanded ed. Washington, DC: National Academy Press.

Brookins, Julia. 2012. "Nationwide Tuning Project for Undergraduate History Programs Launched." *Perspectives on History* 50(3): 14.

Brown, John Seely, Allan Collins, and Paul Duguid. 1989. "Situated Cognition and the Culture of Learning." *Educational Researcher* 18(1): 32–42.

Burkholder, J. Peter. 2011. "Decoding the Discipline of Music History for Our Students." *Journal of Music History Pedagogy* 1(2): 93–111.

Calder, Lendol. 2006. "Uncoverage: Toward a Signature Pedagogy for the History Survey." *Journal of American History* 92(4): 1358–70.

Cameron-Bandler, Leslie, and Michael Lebeau. 1986. *The Emotional Hostage: Rescuing Your Emotional Life.* San Rafael, CA: FuturePace.

Chi, Michelene T. H. 2008. "Three Types of Conceptual Change: Belief Revision, Mental Model Transformation, and Categorical Shift." In *International Handbook of Research on Conceptual Change,* edited by Stella Vosniadou, 61–82. Hillsdale, NJ: Erlbaum.

Chick, Nancy L. 2009. "Unpacking a Signature Pedagogy in Literary Studies." In *Exploring Signature Pedagogies: Approaches to Teaching Disciplinary Habits of Mind,* edited by Regan A. R. Gurung, Nancy L. Chick, and Aeron Haynie, 36–55. Sterling, VA: Stylus.

Cook-Sather, Allison, Catherine Bovill, and Peter Felten. 2014. *Engaging Students as Partners in Learning and Teaching: A Guide for Faculty.* San Francisco: Jossey-Bass.

Currie, Genevieve. Forthcoming. "Conscious Connections: Phenomenology and Decoding the Disciplines." In *Using the Decoding the Disciplines Framework for Learning across Disciplines,* edited by Janice Miller-Young and Jennifer Boman. *New Directions for Teaching and Learning,* forthcoming.

Díaz, Arlene, Joan Middendorf, David Pace, and Leah Shopkow. 2007. "Making Thinking Explicit: A History Department Decodes Its Discipline." *National Teaching and Learning Forum* 16(2): 1–4.

———. 2008. "The History Learning Project: A Department 'Decodes' Its Students." *Journal of American History* 94(4): 1211–24.

Díaz, Arlene, and Leah Shopkow. 2014, July 10. "A Tale of Two Thresholds." Paper presented at the Fifth Biennial International Threshold Concepts Conference, Durham University.

Donald, Janet Gail. 2002. *Learning to Think: Disciplinary Perspectives.* San Francisco: Jossey-Bass.

Durisen, Richard H., and Catherine A. Pilachowski. 2004. "Decoding Astronomical Concepts." In *Decoding the Disciplines: Helping Students Learn Disciplinary Ways of Thinking,* edited by David Pace and Joan Middendorf. *New Directions in Teaching and Learning* 98: 33–44.

Erkan, Ali. 2015, October 28. "Decoding in the Stem Disciplines: Helping Students through Paradigm Shifts in Computer Science." Annual Meetings of the International Society for the Scholarship of Teaching and Learning, Melbourne.

Erekson, Keith. 2011. "Putting History Teaching 'In Its Place.'" *Journal of American History* 7(4): 1067–78.

Felten, Peter. 2013. "Principles of Good Practice in SoTL." *Teaching and Learning Inquiry: The ISSOTL Journal* 1(1): 121–25.

Frederick, Peter. 1995. "Walking on Eggs: Mastering the Dreaded Diversity Discussion." *College Teaching* 43(3): 83–92.

German, Adrian, Joan Middendorf, David Pace, Ali Erkan, Erika Lee, Suzanne Menzel, and John F. Duncan. 2015, October 28. "Decoding in the STEM Disciplines: from Threshold Concepts to Bottlenecks." Annual Meetings of the International Society for the Scholarship of Teaching and Learning, Melbourne.

Graff, Gerald, and Cathy Birkenstein. 2006. *They Say/I Say: The Moves That Matter in Academic Writing.* New York: Norton.

Grim, Valerie, David Pace, and Leah Shopkow. 2004. "Learning to Use Evidence in the Study of History." In *Decoding the Disciplines: Helping Students Learn Disciplinary Ways of Thinking,* edited by David Pace and Joan Middendorf. *New Directions in Teaching and Learning* 98: 57–65.

Grossman, James. 2012. "Tuning In to the History Major." *Perspectives on History* 50(4): 7–8.

Hake, Richard R. 1998. "Interactive-Engagement versus Traditional Methods: A Six-Thousand-Student Survey of Mechanics Test Data for Introductory Physics Courses." *American Journal of Physics* 66(1): 64–74.

Haney, Sally. 2015. "Interrogating Our Past Practice as We Scale the Walls of the Box We Call Journalism Education." http://ryersonjournalism.ca/toward-2020-interrogating

-our-past-practice-as-we-scale-the-walls-of-the-box-we-call-journalism
-education/.

Horowitz, Helen Lefkowitz. 1987. *Campus Life: Undergraduate Culture from the End of the Eighteenth Century to the Present.* New York: Knopf.

Huber, Mary Taylor, and Pat Hutchings. 2005. *The Advancement of Learning: Building the Teaching Commons.* San Francisco: Jossey-Bass.

Huber, Mary Taylor, and Sherwyn P. Morreale. 2002. "Situating the Scholarship of Teaching and Learning: A Cross-Disciplinary Conversation." In *Disciplinary Styles in the Scholarship of Teaching and Learning: Exploring Common Ground,* edited by Mary Taylor Huber and Sherwyn P. Morreale, 1–24. Washington, DC: American Association for Higher Education and the Carnegie Foundation for the Advancement of Learning.

Hutchings, Pat, ed. 1998. *The Course Portfolio: How Faculty Can Examine Their Teaching to Advance Practice and Improve Student Learning.* Washington, DC: American Association for Higher Education.

———. 2007. "Theory: The Elephant in the Scholarship of Teaching and Learning Room." *International Journal for the Scholarship of Teaching and Learning* 1(1): http://digitalcommons.georgiasouthern.edu/ij-sotl/vol1/iss1/2/.

Hutchings, Pat, Mary Taylor Huber, and Anthony Ciccone. 2011. "Getting There: An Integrative Vision of the Scholarship of Teaching and Learning." *International Journal for the Scholarship of Teaching and Learning* 5(1). http://digitalcommons .georgiasouthern.edu/ij-sotl/vol5/iss1/31.

Hyde, Anne. 2012. "Defining Learning Expectations." *Inside Higher Ed,* December 21. https://www.insidehighered.com/views/2012/12/21/essay-how-historians-are-defining-what-students-need-learn.

Immordino-Yang, Mary Helen. 2011. "Implications of Affective and Social Neuroscience for Educational Theory." *Educational Philosophy and Theory* 43(1): 98–103.

Kehm, Barbara, "Quality in European Higher Education: The Influence of the Bologna Process." *Change: The Magazine of Higher Education* 42 (May–Jun 2010), 40–46.

Kurfiss, Joanne Gainen. 1988. "Critical Thinking: Theory, Research, Practice, and Possibilities." *ASHE-ERIC Higher Education Report,* No. 2

Kurz, Lisa, and Trudy W. Banta. 2004. "Decoding the Assessment of Student Learning." In *Decoding the Disciplines: Helping Students Learn Disciplinary Ways of Thinking*" edited by David Pace and Joan Middendorf. *New Directions in Teaching and Learning* 98: 85–94.

Lage, Maureen J., Glenn J. Platt, and Michael Treglia. 2000. "Inverting the Classroom: A Gateway to Creating an Inclusive Learning Environment." *Journal of Economic Education* 31(1): 30–43.

Lahm, Swantje, and Svenja Kaduk. 2016. "'Decoding the Disciplines': ein Ansatz für forschendes Lernen und Lehren." In *Forschendes Lernen. Ein Praxisbuch,* edited by Harald A. Mieg & Judith Lehmann. FHP-Verlag.

Land, Ray, Glynnis Cousin, Jan Meyer, and Peter Davies. 2006. "Implications of Threshold Concepts for Course Design and Evaluation." In *Overcoming Barriers to Student Understanding: Threshold Concepts and Troublesome Knowledge,* edited by Jan Meyer and Ray Land, 195–206. London: Routledge.

Levstik, Linda, and Keith C. Barton. 2002. *Researching History Education: Theory, Method, and Context.* New York: Routledge.

Linkon, Sherry Lee. 2011 *Literary Learning: Teaching the English Major.* Bloomington: Indiana University Press.

MacDonald, Ron. Forthcoming. "Intuitions and Instincts: Considerations for Decoding Disciplinary Identities." In *Using the Decoding the Disciplines Framework for Learning across Disciplines,* edited by Janice Miller-Young and Jennifer Boman. *New Directions for Teaching and Learning,* forthcoming.

Magolda, Marcia Baxter, and Patricia M. King, eds. 2004. *Learning Partnerships: Theory and Models of Practice to Educate for Self-Authorship.* Sterling, VA: Stylus.

Marshall, David W., Michelle Kalina, and Will Dane. 2010. *Tuning Educational Structures: A Guide to the Process.* Indianapolis: Institute for Evidence-Based Change. http://www.iebcnow.org/IEBCPublicFiles/iebc.public/72/72647e6f-d0d4 -4d5f-8997-39d1c1983db4.pdf.

Mehaffey, Rachel, Julie Phillips, Mary Rouse, and Peter Felten. 2015, June 9. "Under-graduate Students Decoding the Disciplines: A SoTL Partnership Studying the Political Science Literature Review." Paper presented at the European Conference on the Scholarship of Teaching and Learning, Cork, Ireland.

Meyer, Jan, and Ray Land. 2003. *Threshold Concepts and Troublesome Knowledge: Linkages to Ways of Thinking and Practising within the Disciplines.* ETL Project Occasional Report 4. Edinburgh: University of Edinburgh. http://www.etl.tla.ed .ac.uk//docs/ETLreport4.pdf.

———. 2005. "Threshold Concepts and Troublesome Knowledge (2): Epistemological Considerations and a Conceptual Framework for Teaching and Learning." *Higher Education* 49(3): 373–88.

———, eds. 2006. *Overcoming Barriers to Student Understanding: Threshold Concepts and Troublesome Knowledge.* London: Routledge.

Michaelsen, Larry K., and Michael Sweet. 2011. "Team-Based Learning." *New Directions for Teaching and Learning* 128: 41–51.

Middendorf, Joan. 1999. "Finding Key Faculty to Influence Change." In *To Improve the Academy: Resources for Faculty, Instructional, and Organizational Development,* vol. 18, edited by Matthew Kaplan and Devorah Lieberman, 83–89. San Francisco: Jossey-Bass.

———. 2004. "Decoding the Disciplines: A Model for Helping Students Learning Disciplinary Ways of Thinking." In *Decoding the Disciplines: Helping Students Learn Disciplinary Ways of Thinking,* edited by David Pace and Joan Middendorf. *New Directions in Teaching and Learning* 98: 1–12.

Middendorf, Joan, and Alan Kalish. 1996. "The 'Change–Up' in Lectures." *TRC Newsletter* 8(1). http://citl.indiana.edu/files/pdf/middendorf_kalish_1996.pdf.

Middendorf, Joan, Jolanta Mickutė, Tara Saunders, José Najar, Andrew E. Clark-Huckstep, and David Pace, with Keith Eberly and Nicole McGrath. 2015. "What's Feeling Got to Do With It? Decoding Emotional Bottlenecks in the History Classroom." *Arts and Humanities in Higher Education* 14: 166–80.

Middendorf, Joan, and David Pace. 2001. "Overcoming Cultural Obstacles to New Ways of Teaching: The Lilly Freshman Learning Project at Indiana University." In *To Improve the Academy: Resources for Faculty, Instructional, and Organizational Development,* vol. 20, edited by Devorah Lieberman and Catherine M. Wehlburg, 208–24. San Francisco: Jossey-Bass.

———. 2004. "Future of Decoding the Disciplines." In *Decoding the Disciplines: Helping Students Learn Disciplinary Ways of Thinking*, edited by David Pace and Joan Middendorf. *New Directions in Teaching and Learning* 98: 109–10.

———. 2007. "Easing Entry into the Scholarship of Teaching and Learning through Focused Assessments: The 'Decoding the Disciplines' Approach." In *To Improve the Academy: Resources for Faculty, Instructional, and Organizational Development*, vol. 26, edited by Douglas Reimondo Robertson and Linda B. Nilson, 53–67. San Francisco: Jossey-Bass.

———. 2010. "Using Just-in-Time Teaching in History." In *Just-in-Time Teaching: Across the Disciplines, across the Academy*, edited by Scott Simkins and Mark Maier, 153–64. Sterling, VA: Stylus.

Middendorf, Joan, and Leah Shopkow "Decoding the Disciplines: How to Help Students Learn Critical Thinking" Unpublished manuscript 2016.

Middendorf, Joan, Leah Shopkow, David Pace, Jim Barnett, and Julie Timmermans. 2014, October 24. "An Accountant, A Geologist, and a Historian Walk into a Bar. . . . Decoding Disciplinary Epistemologies." Panel at the Meeting of the International Society for the Scholarship of Teaching and Learning, Quebec City.

Miller-Young, Janice, and Jennifer Boman. Forthcoming. "Uncovering Ways of Thinking, Practicing and Being through Key Themes in Decoding across Disciplines." In *Using the Decoding the Disciplines Framework for Learning across Disciplines*, edited by Janice Miller-Young and Jennifer Boman. *New Directions for Teaching and Learning*, forthcoming.

———, eds. Forthcoming. *Using the Decoding the Disciplines Framework for Learning across Disciplines. New Directions for Teaching and Learning*, forthcoming.

Miller-Young, Janice, Yasmin Dean, Melanie Rathburn, Jennifer Pettit, Margot Underwood, Judy Gleeson, Roberta Lexier, Victoria Calvert, and Patti Clayton. 2015. "Decoding Ourselves: An Inquiry into Faculty Learning about Reciprocity in Service-Learning." *Michigan Journal of Community Service Learning* 22: 32–47.

Mills, David, and Mary Taylor Huber. 2005. "Anthropology and the Educational 'Trading Zone': Disciplinarity, Pedagogy and Professionalism." *Arts and Humanities in Higher Education* 4: 9–32.

Murphree, Daniel S. 2013. "An Unexpected Bridge: The AHA Tuning Project and Writing across the Curriculum." *Perspectives on History* 51(4). https://www.historians.org/publications-and-directories/perspectives-on-history/april-2013.

Nadler, Susannah. 2012. "Bottlenecks and Threshold Initiative at TLISI." https://blogs.commons.georgetown.edu/blog/archives/1065.

Nelson, C. E. 1999. "On The Persistence of Unicorns: The Tradeoff between Content and Critical Thinking Revisited." In *The Social Worlds of Higher Education: Handbook for Teaching in a New Century*, edited by Bernice A. Pescosolido and Ronald Aminzade, 168–84. Thousand Oaks, CA: Pine Forge.

———. 2012. "Why Don't Undergraduates Really 'Get' Evolution? What Can Faculty Do?" In *Evolution Challenges: Integrating Research and Practice in Teaching and Learning about Evolution*, edited by Karl S. Rosengren, Sarah K. Brem, E. Margaret Evans, and Gale M. Sinatra, 311–47. New York: Oxford University Press.

Neumann, Friederike. 2015. "How Does a Historian Read a Scholarly Text and How Do Students Learn to Do the Same?" In *Enriching History Teaching and Learning:*

Challenges, Possibilities, Practice, edited by David Ludvigsson and Alan Booth, 67–83. Linköping, Sweden: Linköping University. http://liu.diva-portal.org/smash /get/diva2:786270/FULLTEXT01.pdf.

Novak, Gregor. 2010, October 19. "Just-in-Time Teaching and Decoding the Disciplines." Preconference workshop at the Annual Conference of the International Society for the Scholarship of Teaching and Learning, Liverpool, England.

———. 2011. "Just-in-Time Teaching." *New Directions for Teaching and Learning* 128: 63–73.

Novak, Gregor, Andrew Gavrin, Wolfgang Christian, and Evelyn Peterson. 1999. *Just-in-Time Teaching: Blending Active Learning with Web Technology.* Upper Saddle River, NJ: Prentice Hall.

Novak, Gregor, and Evelyn Patterson. 2010. "An Introduction to Just-in-Time Teaching (JiTT)." In *Just-in-Time Teaching: Across the Disciplines, across the Academy,* edited by Scott Simkins and Mark H. Maier, 3–38. Sterling, VA: Stylus.

O'Mahony, Catherine, Avril Buchanan, Mary O'Rourke, and Bettie Higgs, eds. 2014. *Threshold Concepts: From Personal Practice to Communities of Practice. Proceedings of the National Academy's Sixth Annual Conference and the Fourth Biennial Threshold Concepts Conference.* Cork, Ireland: NAIRTL.

Pace, David. 1993. "Beyond 'Sorting': Teaching Cognitive Skills in the History Survey." *History Teacher* 26(2): 211–20.

———. 2003. "Controlled Fission: Teaching Supercharged Subjects." *College Teaching* 51(2): 42–45.

———. 2004. "Decoding the Reading of History: An Example of the Process." In *Decoding the Disciplines: Helping Students Learn Disciplinary Ways of Thinking,* edited by David Pace and Joan Middendorf. *New Directions in Teaching and Learning* 98: 13–21.

———. 2008. "Opening History's 'Black Boxes': Decoding the Disciplinary Unconscious of Historians." In *Teaching and Learning within and beyond Disciplinary Boundaries,* edited by Carolin Kreber, 96–104. London: Routledge.

———. 2011. "Assessment in History: The Case for 'Decoding' the Discipline." *Journal of the Scholarship of Teaching and Learning* 11(3): 107–19.

———. 2012a. "Decoding Historical Evidence." In *Enhancing Student Learning in History: Perspectives on University History Teaching,* edited by David Ludvigsson, 49–62. Uppsala: Swedish Science Press.

———. 2012b. "Prezi and the Decoding of History." In *Quick Hits: Teaching with Technology,* edited by Robin K. Morgan and Kimberly T. Olivares, 91–92. Bloomington: Indiana University Press.

Pace, David, and Joan Middendorf, eds. 2004. *Decoding the Disciplines: Helping Students Learn Disciplinary Ways of Thinking. New Directions in Teaching and Learning* 98.

Pace, David, Janice Miller-Young, Michelle Yeo, Manie Moolman, Jennifer Clark, Adrian Jones, Annette Wilkinson, and Deirdre van Jaarsveldt. 2015, October 28. "Communities of Decoding: Using the Decoding the Disciplines Paradigm to Create Faculty Learning Communities on Three Continents." Panel discussion at the Annual Meetings of the International Society for the Scholarship of Teaching and Learning, Melbourne.

Pace, David, and Sharon Pugh. 1995. *Studying for History.* New York: HarperCollins College.

Perkins, David. 1999. "The Many Faces of Constructivism." *Educational Leadership* 57(3): 6–11.

———. "Constructivism and Troublesome Knowledge." In *Overcoming Barriers to Student Understanding: Threshold Concepts and Troublesome Knowledge,* edited by Jan Meyer and Ray Land, 33–47. London: Routledge.

Perl, Sondra. 2004. *Felt Sense: Writing with the Body.* Portsmouth, NH: Heinemann.

Perry, William G., Jr. 1970. *Forms of Intellectual and Ethical Development in the College Years: A Scheme.* New York: Holt, Rinehart, and Winston.

Pettit, Jennifer, Melanie Rathburn, Victoria Calvert, Roberta Lexier, Margot Underwood, Judy Gleeson, and Yasmin Dean. (accepted). "Building Bridges from the Decoding Interview to Teaching Practice." In *Using the Decoding the Disciplines Framework for Learning Across Disciplines, New Directions for Teaching and Learning,* edited by Janice Miller. In *Using the Decoding the Disciplines Framework for Learning across Disciplines,* edited by Janice Miller-Young and Jennifer Boman. *New Directions for Teaching and Learning* in forthcoming.

Piaget, Jean. 1952. *The Origins of Intelligence in Children.* New York: Norton.

Rubin, M. Barry, and Shanker Krishnan. 2004. "Decoding Applied Data in Professional Schools." In *Decoding the Disciplines: Helping Students Learn Disciplinary Ways of Thinking,* edited by David Pace and Joan Middendorf. *New Directions in Teaching and Learning* 98: 67–73.

Schlegel, Whitney M., and David Pace. 2004. "Using Collaborative Learning Teams to Decode Disciplines: Physiology and History." In *Decoding the Disciplines: Helping Students Learn Disciplinary Ways of Thinking,* edited by David Pace and Joan Middendorf. *New Directions in Teaching and Learning* 98: 75–83.

Schultz, Kyle T., and LouAnn Lovin. 2012. "Examining Mathematics Teachers' Disciplinary Thinking." *Mathematics Educator* 21(2): 2–10.

Shopkow, Leah. 2010. "What 'Decoding the Disciplines' Has to Offer 'Threshold Concepts.'" In *Threshold Concepts and Transformational Learning,* edited by Jan H. F. Meyer, Ray Land, and Caroline Baillie, 317–32. Rotterdam: Sense.

Shopkow, Leah, and Arlene Díaz. 2017. "Of Bottlenecks, Thresholds and Way-Stations." *Teaching and Learning Inquiry,* Forthcoming.

Shopkow, Leah, Arlene Díaz, Joan Middendorf, and David Pace. 2013a. "From Bottlenecks to Epistemology: Changing the Conversation about History in Colleges and Universities." In *Changing the Conversation about Higher Education,* edited by Robert J. Thompson, 15–37. Lanham, MD: Rowman and Littlefield.

———. 2013b. "The History Learning Project 'Decodes' a Discipline: The Marriage of Research and Teaching." In *SoTL in and across the Disciplines,* edited by Kathleen McKinney, 93–113. Bloomington: Indiana University Press.

Shulman, Lee S. 1986. "Those Who Understand: Knowledge Growth in Teaching." *Educational Researcher* 15(2): 4–14.

———. 1993. "Teaching as Community Property: Putting an End to Pedagogical Solitude." *Change: The Magazine of Higher Learning* 25(6): 6–7.

———. 1999. "Taking Learning Seriously." *Change: The Magazine of Higher Learning* 31(4): 10–17.

———. 2002. "Foreword." In *Disciplinary Styles in the Scholarship of Teaching and Learning: Exploring Common Ground,* edited by Mary Taylor Huber and Sherwyn P.

Morreale, v–ix. Washington, DC, American Association for Higher Education and the Carnegie Foundation for the Advancement of Learning.

Simkins, Scott, and Mark H. Maier, eds. 2010. *Just-in-Time Teaching: Across the Disciplines, across the Academy.* Sterling, VA: Stylus.

Sipress, Joel M., and David J. Volker. 2009. "From Learning History to Doing History: Beyond the Coverage Model." In *Exploring Signature Pedagogies: Approaches to Teaching Disciplinary Habits of Mind,* edited by Regan A. R. Gurung, Nancy L. Chick, and Aeron Haynie, 19–35. Sterling, VA: Stylus.

Smith, Michael, and Ali Erkan. 2009, October 25. "Learning History in a Digital Age: Some Experiments with 'Digital Natives.'" Paper presented at the Annual Meeting of the International Society for the Scholarship of Teaching and Learning, Bloomington, IN.

Somers, Caroline. 2014. "Decoding the Discipline for Postgraduate Law Students." http://icep.ie/wp-content/uploads/2014/09/Decoding-the-Discipline-CSOMERS.pdf.

Springer, Leonard, Mary Elizabeth Stanne, and Samuel S. Donovan. 1999. "Effects of Small-Group Learning on Undergraduates in Science, Mathematics, Engineering, and Technology: A Meta-Analysis." *Review of Educational Research* 69(1): 21–51.

Sundt, Jody. 2010. "Overcoming Student Resistance to Learning Research Methods: An Approach Based on Decoding Disciplinary Thinking." *Journal of Criminal Justice Education* 21(3): 266–84.

Sweet, Michael, and Larry K. Michaelsen. 2012. "Critical Thinking and Engagement: Creating Cognitive Apprenticeships with Team-Based Learning." In *Team-Based Learning in the Social Sciences and Humanities: Group Work That Works to Generate Critical Thinking and Engagement,* edited Michael Sweet and Larry K. Michaelsen, 5–32. Sterling, VA: Stylus.

Timmermans, Julie A. 2010. "Changing Our Minds: The Developmental Potential of Threshold Concepts." In *Threshold Concepts and Transformational Learning,* edited by Jan H. F. Meyer, Ray Land, and Caroline Baillie, 3–19. Rotterdam: Sense.

Tobias, Shelia. 1992–93. "Disciplinary Cultures and General Education: What Can We Learn from Our Learners?" *Teaching Excellence* 4(6): 1–3.

Vye, Nancy J., Daniel L. Schwartz, John D. Bransford, Brigid J. Barron, and Linda Zech. 1998. "SMART Environments That Support Monitoring, Reflection, and Revision." In *Metacognition in Educational Theory and Practice.* Edited by Douglas J. Hacker, John Dunlosky, and Arthur C. Graesser. Mahwah, NJ: Erlbaum, 305–46.

Vygotsky, L. S. 1978. *Mind in Society: The Development of Higher Psychological Processes.* Cambridge, MA: Harvard University Press.

Wiggins, Grant, and Jay McTighe. 1998. *Understanding by Design.* Alexandria, VA: Association for Supervision and Curriculum Development.

Wineburg, Sam. 2001. *Historical Thinking and Other Unnatural Acts: Charting the Future of Teaching the Past.* Philadelphia: Temple University Press.

Wineburg, Sam, Mark Smith, and Joel Breakstone. 2015. "Beyond the Bubble: A New Generation of History Assessments." http://beyondthebubble.stanford.edu/.

Woodhouse, Rosamund A. 2010. "Hype or Hope: Can the Scholarship of Teaching and Learning Fulfill Its Promise?" *International Journal for the Scholarship of Teaching and Learning* 4(1). http://digitalcommons.georgiasouthern.edu/ij-sotl/vol4/iss1/13.

Yeo, Michelle. Forthcoming. "Decoding the Disciplines as Hermeneutic Practice." In *Using the Decoding the Disciplines Framework for Learning across Disciplines*, edited by Janice Miller-Young and Jennifer Boman. *New Directions for Teaching and Learning*, forthcoming.

Yeo, Michelle, Mark Lafave, Khatija Westbrook, Dennis Valdez, and Breda Eubank. Forthcoming. "Impact of Decoding Work within a Professional Program." In *Using the Decoding the Disciplines Framework for Learning across Disciplines*, edited by Janice Miller-Young and Jennifer Boman. *New Directions for Teaching and Learning*, forthcoming.

Young, Kathleen McCarthy, and Gaea Leinhardt. 1998. "Writing from Primary Documents." *Written Communication* 15(1): 25–68.

Zhu, Chen, George Rehrey, Brooke Treadwell, and Claudia C. Johnson. 2012. "Looking Back to Move Ahead: How Students Learn Deep Geological Time by Predicting Future Environmental Impacts." *Journal of College Science Teaching* 41(3): 61–66.

Zolan, Miriam, Susan Strome, and Roger Innes. 2004. "Decoding Genetics and Molecular Biology. In *Decoding the Disciplines: Helping Students Learn Disciplinary Ways of Thinking*," edited by David Pace and Joan Middendorf. *New Directions in Teaching and Learning* 98: 23–32.

Index

DAVID PACE

is emeritus professor in the
Department of History at
Indiana University, where he
taught European history for forty
years. A graduate of Rice and
Yale Universities, he is a fellow
at the Carnegie Endowment's
Academy for the Scholarship
of Teaching and Learning, a
recipient of the American
Historical Association's Eugene
Asher Award for Distinguished
Teaching, and the president of
the International Society for the
Scholarship of Teaching and
Learning in History. He was
cofounder of the Indiana
University Freshman Learning
Project and one of the directors
of the History Learning Project.

CPSIA information can be obtained
at www.ICGtesting.com
Printed in the USA
LVOW11s1713101217
559294LV00004B/680/P